MASTE]

MW01078307

SONY A7RV

CAMERA

A step by step beginners operational guide

Joseph Wealth

Contents

INTRODUCTION

Congratulations on your acquisition and welcome to the new Sony Alpha 7R V camera operational user guide.

Sony's Alpha's camera system have advanced greatly in the 3 years since its previous, then A7R IV, was introduced. The new Alpha 7RV hasn't only caught up with, but also outperformed, the rest cameras in the system.

Sony has long stated that the "R" in A7R V stands for "resolution," and prior generations of the camera sacrificed focusing speed for resolution.

Autofocus & Performance Review

The 61-megapixel Exmor R CMOS image sensor in a7RV is identical to that found in a7RIV, however the a7RV employs the newer twin BIONX XR processors seen in the a1 & a7SIII. Sony claims that the new CPU improves imaging quality & performance while also allowing the camera to take 60MP photographs at 10 frames/second.

The new focusing mechanism is a significant improvement in Sony's autofocus performance, putting the a7RV ahead of Sony's previous cameras. Sony is the first one to perfect eye focusing in full-frame mirrorless cameras, first with Eye AF, and then with RealTime Tracking, and the company obviously hopes that this new autofocus technology will be the next great step.

Tilting Screen

The LCD screen is the most contentious camera component. Because of its new four-axis LCD screen, the a7R V should address this issue. The new design has both a tilt and a flip screen, which should put a stop to the ongoing argument. I've called it "the flippy tilty screen."

Autofocus

The a7R V outperforms the a7RIV in autofocus, although that's not saying much considering the a7R IV's notoriously low performance in this field.

The a7R V now features by far the finest focusing system in Sony's portfolio, thanks to its brand-new AI-based autofocus plus dedicated AI Processor that Sony claims was taught using deep learning techniques. The upgraded AI processor allows the a7R V to follow a broader variety of subjects and includes human stance recognition into AF calculations.

According to Sony, the focusing system can now distinguish more birds and animals' heads, eyes, and bodies. It can also detect insects as well as the flanks of vehicles such as automobiles, trains, and aircraft. In my examination, I discovered these claims to be true, and the a7R V's focusing is far superior than that of the a7RIV and every other Sony camera.

I witnessed rapid focusing even at the outer edges of the frame with 693 AF points and broad autofocus coverage, and concluded that the new approach resulted in a greatly improved experience.

Birds

When photographing birds, for instance, I found the focusing to be quite precise and persistent. Flying Birds against clouds have always been difficult to capture, specifically whenever the birds are moving swiftly and far away.

I took my camera device to a raptor viewing area and photographed several kestrels, hawks, and vultures. The autofocus latched on instantaneously and tracked so consistently that my joyful cursing startled a birdwatcher. It also tracked birds at the very edge of the picture in a manner that prior Sony cameras did not. Anybody who phtographed birds or aircraft knows how fast they can move and how crucial tracking is around the edges.

Animals

This autofocus is arguably more prevalent than bird autofocus (hello, cats!), and new Sony cameras perform well with animals, particularly the cats and dogs we hold as pets.

The disparity between both the eyeball as well as the surrounding fur color was quite significant in all of the animals. I shot not just my kitties to put the a7RV to the test, However, there are some sheep.

Why are sheep used? Sheep, despite their leisurely movement, are difficult to focus on. In order to have greater peripheral vision, herd animals have their eyes placed further back on the skull than predators, whose eyes appear forward-faced and easier to spot. Sheep eyes are extremely difficult to detect. However, the a7RV did capture it

Trains

I brought the camera to picture high-speed trains at a local local railway station, where Amtrack lines operate at speeds of up to 100 mph once every hours. I've never had any trouble photographing trains since their huge boxy form makes them an easy subject. However, even as the train rushed at me, the a7RV was able to lock onto the engine's glass, and more significantly, it did not transfer focus to other persons on the track nearby.

Insects

Insect AF also performed as expected. Autofocus systems are used to barely locking onto tiny, fast-moving bugs, however the a7RV system latched onto and followed bees as they took flight and landed. I spent a long time shooting a bee attempting to lift an item from a piece of metal, and the camera highlighted the insect in every single frame, rarely jumping to the shining material it was on.

People

As a long-time bike racing photographer, I understand how difficult it may be to capture an image with a cyclist's face in perfect focus. Autofocus systems are frequently thrown off by helmets and spectacles, and the focus points frequently hop to trees or vertical structures behind the racers.

Despite the speed, the a7R V reliably locked onto bikers' faces. This is probably likely because of the new human posture recognition technology. While focusing systems are unfamiliar with helmets and sunglasses, a biker is a clear and apparent exhibition of moving body components. The entire body is visible, including the shoulders, head, elbows, arms, legs, knees, and feet. These crucial focus points improved the autofocus system's accuracy on bikers more than any other system I've tried. It was so precise that I switched to pans at 1/40 sec or lower and achieved spot-on focusing on the face, which is the pinnacle of any motorcycle shot.

Here's a brief rundown of the top features

- AI-driven Real-Time Recognition Autofocus
- "Tilty Flippy Screen.
- Claimed Eight-stop image stabilization system
- Multiple raw file formats, including lossless raw, compressed raw, and three raw sizes plus JPEG and HEIF
- Dual CFe-A card slots
- 10fps capture
- 583 image burst depth in compressed raw, 547 in uncompressed raw, and more than 1000 images in JPEG X-Fine
- 9.44M dot EVF, which is best in class
- Video capture is possible up to 8K 24/25p and 4K 50/60p in 4:2:2: 10-bit All-I. T
- Pixel Shift capture with the ability to merge images with motion between frames
- Dedicated Still/Video/S&Q mode dial
- Breathing compensation support, focus mapping, and all the latest video tools Sony offers
- UVC/UAC streaming over USB with the ability to record internally simultaneously
- Wi-Fi 802.11 ac 2X2 MIMO
- SuperSpeed USB 10Gbps over USB 3.2 Gen 2

IMPORTANT NOTES BEFORE USING YOUR NEW CAMERA

Unless otherwise specified, the specifications and performance statistics in the handbook are based on an ambient temperature of 77°F (250C) at all times, unless otherwise noted.

Regarding battery packs, data is based on fully charged packs until the charge indicator turns off.

About operating temperatures

It is not suggested to shoot in very hot or cold settings that exceed the camera's working temperature range. Extreme ambient temperatures cause the camera's temperature to increase rapidly. As the temperature of the camera increases, the image quality may degrade. It is recommended to wait till the temperature lowers before beginning the shot.

Depending on the battery and temperature of the camera, the camera may be unable to capture videos or the power may automatically shut off to protect the camera. A notice would be shown on the screen prior to the power being turned off or the inability to record movies. In such instances, the power should be turned off and the battery and camera temperatures allowed to decrease. If the power is switched on before the battery and camera have fully cooled, the power may go out again, or you may be unable to capture videos.

Notes about filming 4K films or for prolonged periods of time

In low-temperature settings, recording duration may be lower, particularly when filming 4K films. The battery pack should be heated or replaced with a fresh one.

Regarding playing movies on various devices

XAVC S and XAVC HS video files can only be viewed on supported devices.

Remarks about recording

Prior to recording, do test recordings to confirm that the camera is functioning correctly.

Playback of images captured with your product on other devices is not guaranteed, nor is playback of images modified or captured with other devices on your device.

Sony cannot make guarantees in the event of damage to or loss of recorded audio data or photos, or failure to record, as a consequence of a malfunction of the recording medium or camera, etc. Therefore, it is suggested that you create a backup of your vital data.

Once the memory card is formatted, all data stored on it will be deleted forever. Before formatting, it is necessary to copy the data to another device or computer.

To duplicate memory cards

In the following scenarios, data might get corrupted. Ensure the data is backed up for safety purposes. During a write or read process, whenever the memory card is removed, the USB cable is unplugged, or the camera is turned off. Whenever the memory card is used in environments with electrical interference or static electricity.

Database file error

When a memory card without an image database file is placed into the camera and the power is switched on, the camera automatically creates an image database using a portion of the memory card's capacity. The procedure may take some time, and the product cannot be utilized until the process is complete.

If a database file problem occurs, all photographs must be exported to a computer, and then the camera's memory card must be formatted.

Do not store or use the camera in the following locations:

1. In regions that are exceptionally cold, humid, or hot. In locations such as a vehicle parked in the sun, the camera body may get distorted, leading to a malfunction.

2. Storing in close proximity to heaters or in bright sunlight. The camera's body might become misshapen or discoloured, which could lead to a malfunction.

3. In areas susceptible to swaying vibration

It might result in faults and an inability to capture data. Moreover, the recording medium may become useless, and the data may get damaged.

4. Near locations with intense magnetic activity

5. In dusty or sandy environments. Dust and sand should not be allowed to enter the camera. This may cause the product to malfunction, and in certain cases, the problem may be permanent.

6. In regions characterized by excessive humidity. This may result in the lens becoming shaped.

In areas where intense radiation or radio waves are emitted. Playback and recording functionality may be compromised.

About moisture condensation

Moisture may condense on the camera's exterior or inside if it is transported immediately from a cold to a warm environment. This moisture condensation may cause the product to malfunction.

To prevent moisture condensation while transferring a camera from a cold to a warm environment, put the camera within an airtight plastic bag before transporting it. Wait about one hour for the product's temperature to reach room temperature.

If moisture condensation occurs, switch off the device and wait one hour for the moisture to dissipate. Remember that trying to snap photographs with moisture remaining on the lens will result in the capture of blurry photos.

Precautions for transporting

Do not strike, hold, or apply excessive force to the following components, if your product is equipped with them:

- The optics
- The Movable monitor
- Transient flash
- Movable viewfinder

Do not raise the camera while it is attached to a tripod. This might result in the socket hole of the tripod fracturing.

Do not sit on chairs or on other surfaces with the camera in the back pocket of your skirt or pants, since this may cause damage or malfunction.

Notes on the product's handling

Check the alignment of the terminal before attaching the cable to it. The cable should then be inserted straight. Do not remove or insert the cable with force. This might result in the terminal breaking.

The camera utilizes magnetic components, including magnets. Diskettes and credit cards are susceptible to magnetism and should not be brought near the camera.

The captured picture may differ from the image seen before recording.

For cameras with a built-in lens Always attach the lens cap while not using the camera. (On versions that have a lens cap)

Compatible with interchangeable-lens cameras. Always attach the lens body cap or front cap while not using the camera. Before attaching the body cap to the product, dust should be removed from the body cap to avoid debris or dust from entering the product.

If the product becomes soiled after usage, it should be cleaned. The presence of salt, dust, sand, water, etc. within the camera may cause a problem.

Utilizing the lenses

When using a power zoom lens, exercise care to avoid getting your fingers or other objects trapped in the lens. (Applicable to models with interchangeable lenses or powered zoom)

If the product must be put under a light source such as sunlight, attach the lens cover. (For interchangeable-lens cameras or versions that have lens covers)

If a bright light source or sunlight reaches the product via its lens, it may concentrate within the device and produce a fire or smoke. The lens cap should be attached while storing the camera. When photographing with backlighting, the sun must be maintained enough away from the viewing angle. Note that flames or smoke may develop even if the light source is significantly distant from the viewing angle.

The lens should not be exposed directly to laser beams. In addition to damaging the image sensor, this may also cause the device to malfunction.

If the subject is near, fingerprints or dust on the lens may appear in the picture. The lens need to be cleaned with a soft cloth, etc.

Regarding the flash (For models with flash)

Keep your fingertips away from the flash. The component that produces light may get heated.

All dirt must be cleaned from the surface of the flash. As a consequence of the heat generated by the light emission, dirt on the surface of the flash may burn or create smoke. The surface should be cleaned using a gentle substance to remove any dust or grime.

After usage, the flash should be returned to its original position. Ensure that the flash is not protruding. (Applicable to models with a moveable flash).

Concerning the Multi Interface Shoe (For models having a Multi Interface Shoe)

Prior to disconnecting or attaching accessories like as an external flash from the Multi Interface Shoe, the power must be turned OFF. Ensure that the accessory is securely fastened to the product while attaching it.

Do not use the Multi Interface Shoe with commercially available flashes that apply voltages of 250 V or greater or have a polarity opposite to that of the camera. It might lead to a malfunction.

Regarding the flash and lens (For models with flash or viewfinder)

Use care so your finger does not get in the way when the flash or viewfinder button is pressed. (For versions with an adjustable flash or viewfinder).

Sand, dust, or water accumulating on the flash unit or viewfinder may cause a malfunction. (For cameras with a moveable flash or viewfinder)

Regarding the viewfinder (For models with viewfinders)

When using the viewfinder to take photographs, you may suffer nausea, motion sickness, weariness, or eyestrain. We recommend taking pauses at regular intervals anytime you are shooting via a viewfinder.

If you experience discomfort, discontinue use of the viewfinder until your condition improves, and if necessary, see a physician.

When drawing out the eyepiece, do not forcefully press the viewfinder down. It might lead to a malfunction. (For versions with retractable eyepieces and a moveable viewfinder)

If the camera is panned while looking through the viewfinder, or if your eyes move, the image in the viewfinder may become distorted or its color may change.

This is a characteristic of the display device or lens, not a defect. When taking photographs, we recommend focusing on the center of the viewfinder.

The image may be somewhat distorted near to the viewfinder's edges. There is no malfunction here. Additionally, the monitor may be utilized to observe the whole composition together its many details.

If the camera is utilized in cold environments, the picture may have a smeared appearance. There is no malfunction here.

Regarding the monitor

Do not press against the screen. The display may get discolored, which may lead to a problem. If water droplets or other liquids are present on the display, wipe it using a soft substance. If the monitor remains wet, its surface may degrade or alter. This might lead to a malfunction.

If the camera is utilized in cold environments, the picture may have a smeared appearance. There is no malfunction here.

When cables are attached to the camera's terminals, the monitor's range of rotation may be restricted.

Regarding the image sensor

If the camera is directed towards an extremely bright source of light while shooting photographs with a low ISO sensitivity, image highlights may be captured as black.

About image data compatibility

This camera adheres to the Design rule for Camera File system (DCF) international standard established by the Japan Electronics and Information Technology Industries Association (JEITA).

Software and services provided by third-party firms

The content, network services, and [operating system in addition to] software of this camera may be subject to certain terms and conditions and may be withdrawn or stopped, altered at any moment, and may need registration, fees, and credit card information.

Connecting to the Internet

To connect the camera to a network, it must be linked through a LAN port or a router with equivalent capabilities. Attempts to connect in a method other than this may result in security difficulties.

About safety

Sony shall not be held liable for any damage caused by the failure to carry out appropriate security measures on the transmission gadgets, inevitable data leaks caused by transmission specifications, or any other security problem.

Unsupported third parties on that network could be able to access the camera, depending on the use circumstances.

When connecting a camera to a network, you must verify that the network is adequately secured.

The contents of your conversations may be intercepted without your awareness by unauthorized third parties in the signal's vicinity. Whenever wireless LAN connection is utilized, adequate security measures must be applied to protect the confidentiality of transmitted data.

FTP functionality

Since ordinary FTP does not encrypt passwords, users, and material, FTPS should be used if available.

Optional accessories

It is advised that you use genuine Sony accessories.

Certain Sony accessories are exclusive to certain areas and countries.

Regarding battery and battery pack charging

Ensure that only genuine Sony battery packs are used.

Under some climatic or operational situations, the real battery life indicator may not be shown.

The battery pack must not come into contact with water. It lacks water resistance.

The pack should not be left in very heated environments, such as direct sunlight or a vehicle.

The (included) battery pack must be charged prior to the first use of the camera.

The charged pack will gradually discharge even if it is not in use. Every time the product is used, the pack should be charged so that photo possibilities are not missed.

Only charge battery packs that are compatible with this camera. This might lead to injuries, burns, electrical shocks, explosions, overheating, or leaks.

When using a brand-new battery pack or one that hasn't been used in a while, the CHARGE (charge bulb) may flash quickly while the battery is being charged. If this occurs, the battery pack must be removed and reinserted to recharge.

We recommend charging the pack at ambient temperatures between 10 and 30 °C (50 and 86 °F). The pack may be incorrectly charged at temperatures outside of this range.

It is not possible to guarantee operation with all external power suppliers.

Once charging is complete, unplug the AC Adaptor from the power socket (wall outlet) or detach the USB cord from the product. Failing to do so may decrease the battery's lifetime.

Do not repeatedly or continuously charge the battery pack without using it if it is already fully or almost fully charged. This may result in a degradation of the battery's performance.

If the camera's charge indicator flashes while charging, the battery pack should be removed and then firmly reinserted. If the charge indicator flashes again, this may indicate that the battery is defective or that a different battery pack was installed.

Verify that the battery pack is of the correct kind. If the pack is the suggested kind, it should be removed, replaced with a different or new one, and the charging status of the freshly inserted battery should be verified. If the freshly inserted battery charges normally, the prior battery may be defective.

If the charge indicator flashes when the AC Adaptor is connected to the camera and the power socket (wall outlet), charging has momentarily ceased and is in standby mode. Whenever the temperature exceeds the recommended working temperature, charging stops and immediately enters standby mode. Once the temperature returns to the acceptable range, charging resumes and the charge is turned back on.

The included AC Adaptor is unique to this camera. Do not link various technological devices. That action might result in a malfunction.

Battery indicator

The remaining battery indicator shows on the screen.

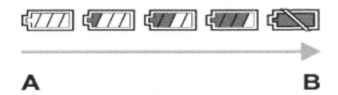

A: The Camera's battery level is high

B: The Cameras battery is exhausted

It takes around one minute for the real battery life indicator to appear.

Under some climatic and operational situations, the real battery life indicator may not be shown.

If the indication does not shown on screen, use the Display Setting (DISP) button to display it.

To properly use the battery pack;

Battery performance decreases in low-temperature conditions. In colder environments, the battery pack has a lower runtime. For a longer battery pack life, we recommend warming it by putting it in your pocket close to your body before inserting it into the device before to shooting. Apply cautious so as not to produce a short circuit if your pockets include metallic things such as keys.

The battery will deplete rapidly if the flash or continuous shooting feature is utilized, the power is often switched on and off, or the monitor's brightness is set to a very high level.

We recommend that you bring additional batteries and do test pictures before shooting the actual photographs.

If the battery terminal becomes soiled, the camera may not turn on or the battery pack may not be fully charged. In such a case, the battery should be cleaned by softly wiping off dust with a cotton swab or a soft cloth.

Putting away the battery pack

In order to protect the functionality of the battery pack, it should be charged and then completely drained in the product at least once a year prior to storage. After removing the battery from the camera, it should be kept in a dry, cold area.

About battery life

The battery's lifespan is limited. The capacity of a battery steadily diminishes as it is used frequently or for lengthy durations. If the battery's usable duration has been drastically reduced, it is likely time to replace it with a new one.

Battery life varies depending on how the pack is stored as well as the climate and operation circumstances of each pack.

Regarding memory card

If (warning symbol for overheating) is shown on the monitor, the memory card should not be removed from the device immediately. Instead, after turning off the camera, the memory card should be ejected after a brief delay. If you touch the memory card while it is hot, you are likely to drop it, resulting in card damage. Use cautious while removing the memory card.

Fragmentation of the data inside a file on the memory card may occur if photographs are erased and captured repeatedly for a lengthy period of time, and video recordings may be interrupted during shooting. If this occurs, save the images to an alternative storage space or a computer, and then perform [Format] on the camera.

Do not remove the memory card or battery pack, disconnect the USB cord, or turn off the device while the access light is on. This might potentially result in data corruption on the memory card.

Ensure the data is backed up for safety purposes.

Not all memory cards are guaranteed to function correctly.

Images stored on a CFexpress Type A/SDXC memory card cannot be viewed or imported on AV devices or PCs incompatible with exFAT when connected via USB connection. Verify that the device supports exFAT before attaching it to the device. If the camera is attached to an incompatible device, you may be prompted to format the card. Never format a card in response to such instructions, since doing so would erase all of its data.

CFexpress Type A and SDXC memory cards utilize the exFAT file system.

Water should not be introduced to the memory card. Avoid dropping, bending, and striking the memory card.

Do not store or use the memory card in the following circumstances:

- Places with high temperatures, such as sun-baked autos parked in the shade
- Locations that get direct sunlight
- Humid locations or locations with corrosive compounds

If the memory card is utilized in close proximity to strong magnetic fields, electrical noise, or static electricity, the data stored on the card may get corrupted.

Do not contact the terminal portion of the memory card with a metallic item or your hand.

The memory card should not be accessible to young children. They may accidentally consume it.

Do not alter or dismantle the memory card.

After prolonged usage, the memory card may get warm. Use cautious while manipulating it.

Memory cards formatted on a computer may not be compatible with the camera. Format the memory card using the provided software.

Data write/read speeds vary depending on the hardware and memory card used.

When writing on the memo area of a memory card, avoid applying excessive pressure.

Label neither the memory card adapter nor the memory card itself. Possible inability to remove the memory card.

If the delete-protect switch or write-protect switch is set to the LOCK position on an SD memory card, photos cannot be erased or recorded. In such circumstances, the record switch should be engaged.

To utilize microSD cards with this camera, you must:

- Ensure that the memory card is inserted into its corresponding adapter. If a memory card is loaded into the camera without an adapter, it may be impossible to remove it.
- When inserting the memory card into its adapter, be sure to enter it in the correct orientation and then push it in as far as possible. If the memory card is improperly installed, a fault may occur.

Sensor Cleansing

If debris or dust enters the camera and adheres to the surface of the image sensor (the component that converts light into an electric signal), it may appear as black spots on the photograph, depending on the environment in which it was taken.

Immediately clean the picture sensor using the instructions below if this occurs.

Ensure that the battery is well charged.

Launch the MENU, choose Setup, click Setup Option, click Anti-Dust Function, click Sensor Cleaning, and then press Enter. The image sensor will vibrate slightly to remove dust.

Removing the lens.

Using blowers that are commercially available, clean the surface of the image sensor and its surrounding region.

The camera should be held with a small downward tilt to encourage dust to fall out.

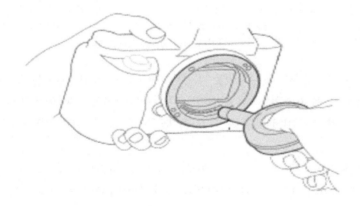

Important

When using the cleaning mode, the lens must be removed while the device is powered on.

Do not switch off the camera when cleaning.

Prior to cleaning, ensure that the remaining battery level is at least three remaining battery icons.

To switch off the camera while cleaning the image sensor, set [Shutter When Pwr OFF] to [Off] under [Anti-dust Function].

Do not use the spray-type blower, as it may disperse water droplets inside the camera's body.

To avoid the blower's tip from contacting the image sensor, do not insert the blower's tip into the opening after the lens mount area.

When using blowers to clean the image sensor, avoid blowing with excessive force. If the sensor is blown too violently, the camera's inside may be compromised.

During the cleaning process, the image sensor emits a vibrating sound. There is no malfunction here.

Cleaning may be conducted automatically upon power off.

During cleaning;

The optics

Do not use cleaning products containing organic solvents such as benzene or thinner.

When cleaning the surface of the lens, dust should be removed using commercially available blowers. In situations of dust adhering to the surface, remove it using lens cleaning solution-moistened tissue paper or soft material. Clean in circular patterns, beginning in the center and working outward. The surface of the lens should not be sprayed directly with lens cleaning solution.

The camera's main body

The camera components inside the lens mount, such as the lens signal contact, must not be disturbed. To remove dust from inside the lens mount, commercially available blowers* should be utilized.

Do not use the spray-type blower, as its usage may cause a malfunction.

The camera's exterior

After wiping the surface of the camera with a wet soft cloth, dry the surface with a dry towel. To prevent damage to the housing or finish:

Avoid exposing the camera to chemical compounds such as pesticide, sunscreen, insect repellent, disposable cloths, alcohol, benzene, and thinner.

Do not contact the camera if you have any of the aforementioned chemicals on your hands.

Do not expose the camera to vinyl or rubber for a lengthy period of time.

The display monitor

If the monitor is cleaned vigorously using tissue paper, etc., it may get scratched.

If the monitor becomes soiled with dust or fingerprints, the dust should be wiped carefully from the surface, and then the monitor should be cleaned with a soft cloth, etc.

ACCESSORIES SUPPLIED

1. The Sony Camera- One piece

2. One piece of shoulder Strap

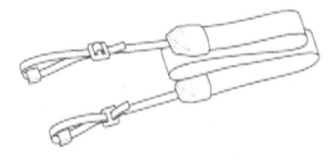

3. The AC Adaptor- One piece

The AC Adaptor varies with countries

4. The Power cord – One piece (mains lead)

Multiple power cables might be provided with the camera. A suitable one matching your region/country should be used

5. One piece of Type-C USB

6. One piece of Battery Pack (rechargeable)

7. One piece of shoe Cap (device connected)

8. One piece of Body Cap (device connected)

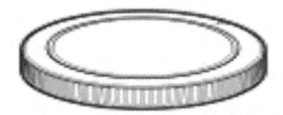

9. One piece of Eyepiece Cup (device connected)

Preferred memory cards

This camera is compatible with SD memory cards (supports UHS-I & UHS-II) and CFexpress Type A memory cards. Whenever microSD memory cards are used with the camera, ensure that an appropriate adaptor is used.

For shooting still-images

The suitable memory cards are as follows.

- Cfexpress Type A memory cards
- SDXC/SDHC/SD memory cards

Record movies

The formats for recording movies as well as the suitable memory cards are below:

▶■ File Format	Maximum recordable bit rate	Supported memory card
XAVC HS 4K	200Mbps	CFexpress Type A memory card SDHC/SDXC card (U3/V30 or higher)*
XAVC S 4K	200Mbps	CFexpress Type A memory card SDHC/SDXC card (U3/V30 or higher)*
XAVC S HD	100Mbps	CFexpress Type A memory card SDHC/SDXC card (U3/V30 or higher)*

XAVC S-I 4K	600Mbps	CFexpress Type A memory card (VPG200 or higher) SDXC V90 or higher
XAVC S-I HD	222Mbps	CFexpress Type A memory card (VPG200 or higher) SDXC V90 or higher

Whenever the recording bitrate is 60 Mbps or below, SDXC/SDHC cards may also be used (Class 10).

Shoot S&Q Motion

The appropriate file formats and memory cards for capturing S&Q Motion Files are listed below.

The bitrate for slow-motion recordings is higher than normal. There may be a need for memory cards with faster writing rates.

▶■ File Format	Maximum recordable bit rate	Supported memory card
XAVC HS 4K	200Mbps	CFexpress Type A memory card (VPG200 or higher) SDXC V60 or higher
XAVC S 4K	200Mbps	CFexpress Type A memory card (VPG200 or higher) SDXC V60 or higher
XAVC S HD	100Mbps	CFexpress Type A memory card SDHC/SDXC card (U3/V30 or higher)*1
XAVC S-I 4K	600Mbps	CFexpress Type A memory card (VPG200 or higher) SDXC V90 or higher*2
XAVC S-I HD	222Mbps	CFexpress Type A memory card (VPG200 or higher) SDXC V90 or higher

Whenever [S&Q Frame Rate] is put to [120fps]/[100fps], [S&Q Rec Frame Rate] is put to [30p]/[25p]/[24p], and the recordable bitrate is put to 50 Mbps, a CFexpress Type A memory card (VPG200 or larger) or an SDXC card (V60 or larger) is needed.

When [**S&Q** Frame Rate] is put to [60fps]/[50fps] and [**S&Q** Rec Frame Rate] is put to [30p]/[25p]/[24p] for slow-mo recording, a CFexpress Type A memory card (VPG200 or larger) is needed.

Important

When shooting proxy movies, higher-speed memory cards might be required.

CFexpress Type B memory cards can't be used.

When SDHC memory cards are used in recording XAVC S movies for long periods of time, the movies recorded would be split into 4 GB files.

When movies are recorded on memory cards in both slots – Slot 1 & Slot 2 – using the camera settings below, insert two cards with similar file systems. Movies can't be simultaneously recorded when a combination of FAT32 and exFAT file systems are used.

Memory card	File system
CFexpress Type A memory card, SDXC memory card	exFAT
SDHC memory card	FAT32

The battery pack should be sufficiently charged before you attempt to get the database files saved to the memory card.

DEVICE LAYOUT

The Front side

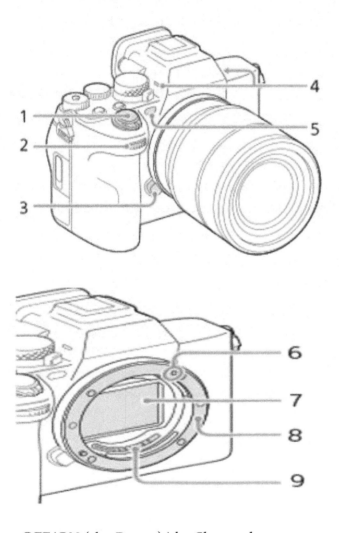

1. OFF/ON (the Power)/the Shutter button

2. The Front dial: Here the settings for each of the shooting modes can be quickly adjusted.

3. The Lens releasing button

4. The Microphone: This part should not be covered while recording movies. Doing that might reduce the volume or cause noise.

5. The Self-timer lamp/ AF illuminator: This part shouldn't be covered during shoots.

6. The Mounting index

7. The Image sensor

8. The Mount

9. The Camera Lens contact

The Rear side

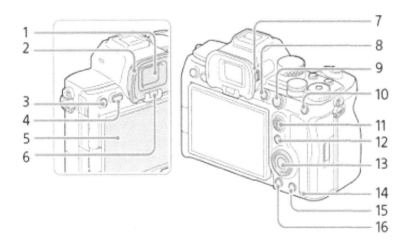

1. The Viewfinder

2. The Eyepiece Cup: In removing the eyepiece cup, the grips at the base of the eyepiece cup should be pushed leftwards and rightwards and the cup lifted.

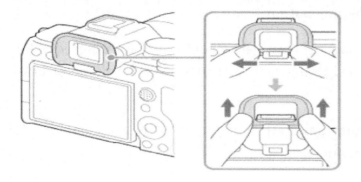

3. Used for shooting: Custom button 3.

Used to view: 🔑 (Secure) button

4. The MENU button

5. Monitor (used in touch operations: Touch pad/Touch panel). The monitor can be adjusted to an angle that is easily viewable and shots taken from any position.

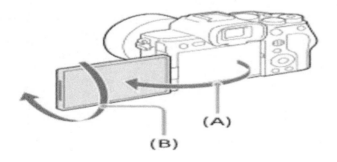

(A)

(B)

- (A): Approximately at an angle 176°
- (B): Approximately at an angle 270°

You might be unable to modify the monitor angle contingent on the kind of tripod used. In such cases, the tripod screw should be released once to alter the monitor angle.

Don't use too much force when rotating, closing, or opening the monitor. Doing that might result in a malfunction.

6. The Eye sensor

7. The Diopter-adjusting dial: The diopter-adjustment dial should be adjusted based on your eyesight till the display clearly shows in the viewfinder. If it's hard to use the diopter-adjustment dial, the eyepiece cup should be removed prior to using the dial.

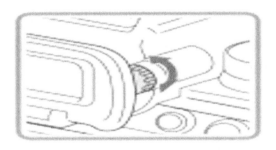

8. Custom button 1

9. Used to shoot: (AF On) button

To view: ⊕ (Enlarger) button

10.   To   shoot: The   AEL   button [AEL hold] is designated to AEL button under default. To view: ▨ (Imaging index) button

11. The Multi-selector

12. To shoot: Fn button

To view: ⤴ (transfer to phone) button

It is possible to show the screen for sending pictures to phones by touching this button.

13. The Control wheel

14. The Access lamp

15. To shoot: C4 button (Custom button 4) To view: 🗑 (Erase) button

16. ▶ (The Playback) button

Adjusting your monitor angle

- While you hold your camera in the low or high position, you should pull your monitor to yourself to modify the angle.

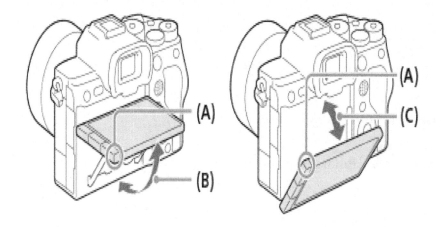

- (A): Position your fingers here
- (B): Approximately 98° from the camera's rear surface.
- (C): Approximately 40° from the camera's rear surface.

Under self-portrait with your monitor, open to the side while the lens is facing you, the image on the monitor will be flipped horizontally. You should rotate your monitor backwards in order to stop the flipped display.

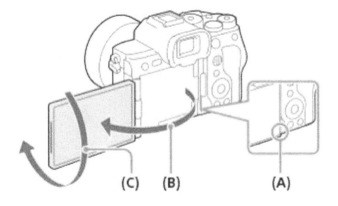

- (A): Position your fingers here
- (B): Approximately 180 degree
- (C): Approximately 270 degree

If you intend to switch the orientation of the display to self-portrait mode while you've pulled out the monitor, you should turn the monitor completely to the (A) direction. If you wish to cancel the orientation of the display for self-portrait mode, then rotate the monitor completely in the (B) direction. (if [Monitor Flip Direction] is adjusted to [Auto]).

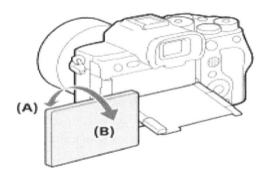

Under default settings, you have the inversion of the camera's display auto turned on & off based on the monitor's positioning. Lock your display method by going to: MENU → then (Setup) → [Finder/Monitor] → then [Monitor Flip Direction].

The Top side

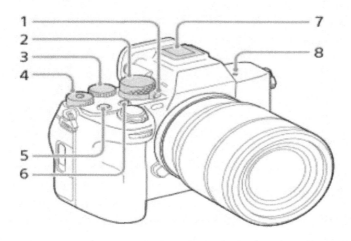

1. Movie/Still/S&Q dial: The shooting mode can be switched. Move the S&Q/Movie/Still dial while pressing the lock release button at the front of the dial.

2. The Mode dial

3. The Rear dial L: The settings for each of these modes can be quickly adjusted.

4. Rear dial R: The settings for each of these modes can be quickly adjusted. Touching the lock button at the middle changes the dial between the unlocked and locked status. The dial is opened when the lock button pops up and the white line is apparent.

5. MOVIE button

6. The Custom button 2

7. The Multi Interface Shoe: Certain accessories might not go to the end and extend backwards from the Multi interface shoe. Nevertheless, when that accessory gets to the shoe's front end, the connection is completed.

8. ⊖ The Image sensing mark position: This sensor transforms light into electric signals. The placement of the image sensor is denoted by ⊖ . When the precise distance between the subject and the camera is measured, check with the placement of the horizontal line.

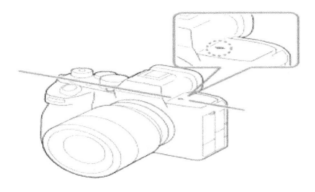

Should the subject be closer compared to the lens' minimum shooting distance, the focus can't be confirmed. Ensure that sufficient distance is put between the camera and the subject.

The Sides

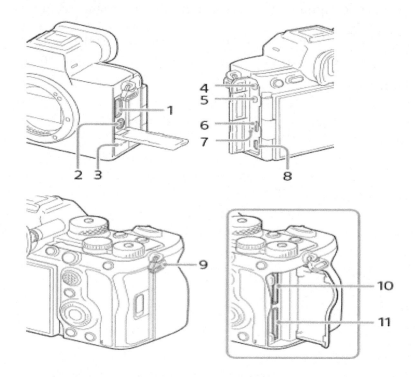

1. The HDMI type A jack

2. ⚡ Flash synchronising terminal

3. The Speaker

4. The (Microphone 🎤) jack: Whenever an external microphone is attached, the inbuilt microphone automatically turns off. If the external mike is the plugin-power type, the microphone's power is provided by the camera.

5. The (Headphones 🎧) jack

6. The Type-C USB terminal

7. The Charge lamp

8. The Micro/Multi/ USB Terminal: This terminal is compatible with devices that are compatible with Micro USB.

9. The shoulder strap Hook: Both ends of the strap should be attached to the camera.

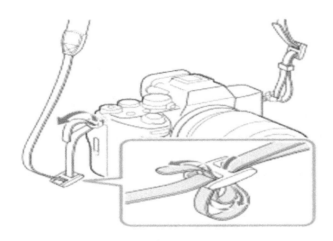

10. The Memory card slot 1

11. The Memory card slot 2

USB terminals

Either the Micro/Multi USB Terminal or the USB Type-C terminal can be used for USB communications. Nevertheless, USB communications cannot be conducted using both terminals at the same time. The USB Type-C terminal should be used to provide power as well as charge the battery pack. This product can't be powered using the Micro/Multi USB terminal.

Accessories can be used for the Micro/Multi USB Terminal, like the remote commander (not included), while providing power or carrying out PC Remote shooting via the USB Type-C terminal.

About the terminal cover

Ascertain that the cover of the terminal is closed prior to use.

Cable protector

You can use your cable protector to avoid the cable from disconnection while shooting images using a connected cable.

Attaching your cable protector

1. Open the cover for HDMI terminal and USB terminal.

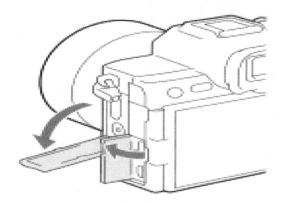

2. Pass the cable protector hook (A) into notch (B) beneath Micro/Multi/USB terminal, then attach it in a way that it covers the camera's terminal surface while you press down to prevent it from falling off.

- Fasten your cable protector to allow the cover of the opened HDMI terminal to be introduced into the cable protector's opening.

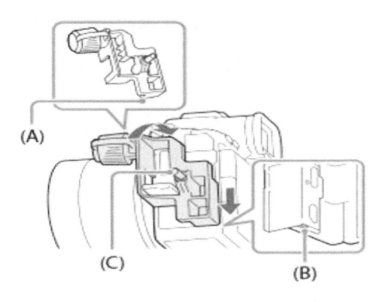

(A)

(C)

(B)

3. Thrust in your attachment screw (C), then twist it to lock your cable protector.

4. Introduce the cable to any of the jacks.

5. Introduce the cable into its holding part, then use the fixing dial (D) to lock the cable.

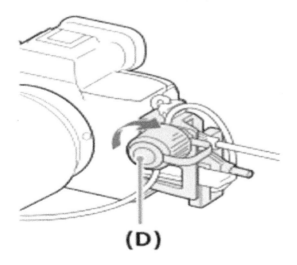

(D)

Removing your cable protector

Release the attaching screw, and remove your cable protector.

The Bottom

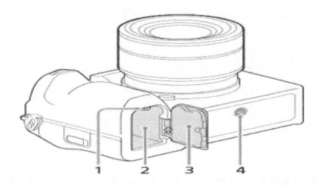

1. The Lock lever

2. The Battery inset slot

3. The Battery cover: When attaching accessories like the vertical grip (not included), the battery cover should be removed.

Removing the battery cover

The release lever for the battery cover (A) should be pulled following the arrow's direction, and afterwards the battery cover removed.

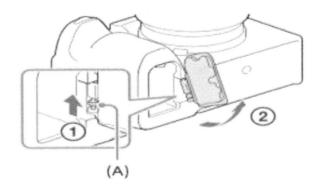

(A)

Attaching the battery cover

The shaft should be inserted at one part of the battery cover into the site of attachment, and afterwards push the battery cover in by connecting the shaft at the opposite part.

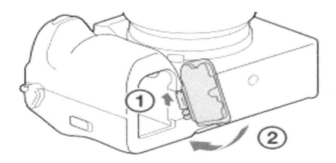

4. The Tripod socket hole: Uses 1/4-20 UNC screws

Tripods with screws lower than 7/32 inches (5.5 mm) long should be used. Otherwise, you'll be unable to firmly attach the camera, and the camera might get damaged.

TOUCH OPERATIONS

Fixes whether touch operations is to be enabled on the monitor or not.

1. MENU → ▣ (Setup) → [Touch Operation] → [Touch Operation] → specific setting.

Menu options

- On: Enables touch operations.
- On: Playback Only: Only enables touch operations during playback.
- Off: Disables touch operations.

Touch Panel/Pad

Touch operations whenever the monitor is used in shooting is known as "touch panel operations," and touch operations whenever the viewfinder is used in shooting is known as "touch pad operations." You could choose whether to enable touch pad operations or touch panel operations.

1. MENU → ▣ (Setup) → [Touch Operation] → [Touch Pad/Panel] → specific setting.

Menu options

- Both Valid: Enables both the touch panel operations whenever shooting is done using the monitor and touch pad operations whenever the viewfinder is used in shooting.

- Touch Panel Only: Only enables the touch panel operations whenever the monitor is used in shooting.

- Touch Pad Only: Only enables the touch pad operations whenever viewfinder is used in shooting.

Touch Pad Settings

Settings associated with touch pad operations can be adjusted when shooting with viewfinder.

1. MENU → ▣ (Setup) → [Touch Operation] → [Touch Pad Settings] → specific setting.

Menu options

- **Operations in a Vertical Alignment/Orientation:** Fixes whether to activate touch pad operations when shooting with vertically oriented viewfinder. You can limit erroneous operations in the course of vertically oriented shooting resulting from your nose, etc. coming in contact with the monitor.

- **Touch Position Mode:** Fixes whether the focusing frame is to be moved to the point tapped on the screen ([Absolute Position]), or the focusing frame moved to the specific point on the basis of the direction of pulling as well as the degree of movement ([Relative Position]).

- **Operation Area:** Fixes the region reserved for touch pad operations. Limiting the operational region can limit erroneous operations resulting from your nose, etc. coming in contact with the monitor.

47

On Touch Positioning Mode

Choosing [Absolute Position] allows the focusing frame to be moved to a far point much quickly because the placement of the focusing frame can be directly specified via touch operations.

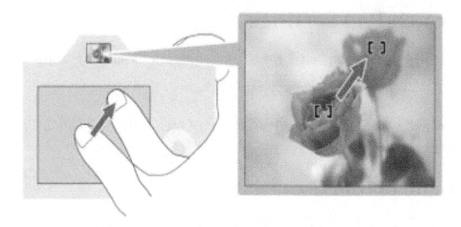

Choosing [Relative Position] allows you use the touch pad from any place that's easiest, without needing to move the finger over wide areas.

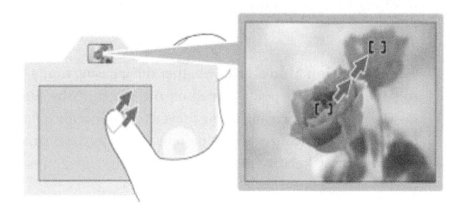

Hint

- Under touch pad operations whenever [Touch Position Mode] is fixed to [Absolute Position], the region fixed in [Operation Area] is considered as the whole screen.

Touch Fn. while Shooting

Fixes the operation enabled by touching the screen when shooting.

1. MENU → ▣ (Setup) → [Touch Operation] → [Touch Func. in Shooting] → specific setting.

Menu options

- **Touch Focus:** The focusing position is fixed by tapping the screen when shooting.

- **Touch Tracking:** The subject is chosen and tracking is began by tapping the screen when shooting.

- **Off:** Deactivates touch operations when shooting.

Hint

- The setting for [Touch Func. in Shooting] can be changed by tapping touch function icon (🖐 / 🖐 / OFF) on the screen for shooting.

Focusing via touch operations –The Touch Focus

[Touch Focus] lets you specify the position to be focused on via touch operations. Choose MENU → 🧰 (Setup) → [Touch Operation] → [Touch Operation] → [On] in advance.

This function is obtainable whenever [📷 Focus Area] is fixed to any of the parameters below:

- [Wide]
- [Zone]
- [Center Fix]
- [Tracking: Wide]
- [Tracking: Zone]
- [Tracking: Center Fix]

1. MENU → 🧰 (Setup) → [Touch Operation] → [Touch Func. in Shooting] → [Touch Focus].

- The setting for [Touch Fn. in Shooting] can be changed by tapping touch function icon (👆 / 👆 / 👆OFF) on the screen for shooting.

To specify the point to be focused on under still image mode

When carrying out auto-focusing, the point to be focused on can be specified via touch operations. After tapping the monitor and outlining a point, focus by partly pressing the shutter button down.

1. Tap the monitor.

- When the monitor is used in shooting, tap the point to be focused on.
- When the viewfinder is used in shooting, the point of focus can be moved by tapping and pulling on the monitor while watching through the viewfinder.

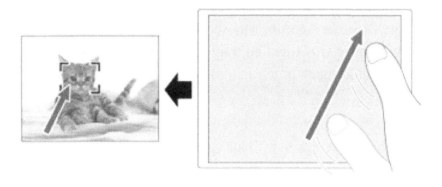

To disable focusing via touch operations, tap 🖐✕ (Touch focus release) symbol or touch the middle of the control wheel when the monitor is used in shooting, and touch the middle of the control wheel if the viewfinder is used in shooting.

2. Partly push the shutter button down to focus.

- Shoot images by fully pressing the shutter button down.

51

To specify the point to be focused on under the movie recording mode

The product focuses on the subject touched.

1. Tap the subject to be focused on prior to or during recording.

- Whenever [▶📷 Focus Mode] is fixed to [Continuous AF], the focus mode temporarily changes to manual focus, making it possible to adjust the focus via the focus ring (spot focus). Spot focus is unavailable when the viewfinder is used in shooting.

- To disable spot focus, tap ⌐👆⌐× (Touch focus release) symbol or push the middle of the control wheel.

- Whenever [▶📷 Focus Mode] is fixed to [Manual Focus], the focus mode temporarily changes to [Continuous AF]. Whenever the touched region is under focus, the focus mode goes back to manual focus.

Hint

- Alongside the touch focus function, touch operations like below are also obtainable.

- The focusing frame for [Expand Spot] and [Spot] can be moved by pulling.

- When capturing still images under manual focusing mode, the focus magnifier could be used by tapping the monitor twice.

Note

The touch focus function is unavailable in the situations below:

- When capturing still images under manual focusing mode
- Whenever digital zoom is in use
- Whenever LA-EA4 is in use

To start tracking using touch operations (Touch Tracking)

Touch operations can be used to choose the subject to be tracked under the movie recording mode and the still image shooting mode.

Choose MENU → 🧰 (Setup) → [Touch Operation] → [Touch Operation] → [On] beforehand.

1. MENU → 🧰 (Setup) → [Touch Operations] → [Touch Fn. while Shooting] → [Touch Tracking].

Settings for [Touch Func. in Shooting] can be changed by tapping touch function symbol (👆 / 👆 / 👆OFF) on the screen for shooting.

2. Tap the subject to be tracked on the monitor.

Tracking will begin.

Whenever the viewfinder is used in shooting, the touch pad can be used to choose the subject to be tracked.

Hint

To disable tracking, tap Tracking release (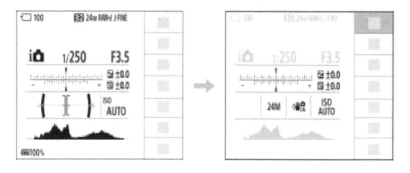...) symbol or push the middle of the control wheel.

Note

[Touch Tracking] isn't available in the situations below:

- Whenever [🄰 Focus Mode] is fixed to [Manual Focus].
- Whenever the Digital Zoom, Clear Image Zoom, and Smart Zoom is in use

If the focus mode is changed to [Manual Focus] while [Touch Fn. in Shooting] is fixed to [Touch Tracking], setting values for [Touch Fn. in Shooting] would be altered to [Touch Focus].

Use the Function button on the [For viewfinder] display

If the Function button is pressed with the monitor display set to [For viewfinder], the items to be changed can be directly operated.

Under automatic mode

Under P/A/S/M mode

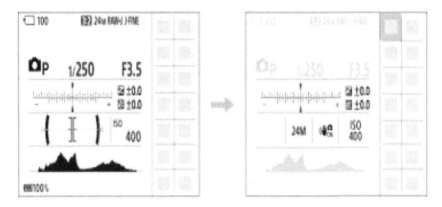

The contents displayed as well as their positions displayed in the illustrations are simply a guideline, and might differ from the real display.

Adjusting your settings using the target setting screens

Choose the symbol for the needed function and afterwards touch the middle of the control wheel. The specific setting screen for that function will show. Adjust the settings by following the operating guide (A).

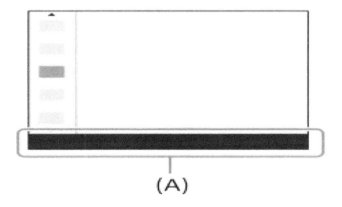

(A)

Important

- Items grayed-out on the [For viewfinder] screen can't be altered by using the Fn button.

- Certain settings, like [ Picture Profile] and [🎬 Creative Look], can't be executed on the [For viewfinder] screen except the specific setting screen is entered.

Monitor

By touching the display, intuitive functions like as focusing on the shooting screen and controlling the playback screen may be done.

Shooting screen

Touch the display to indicate the area of interest (Touch Focus). Touching the subject on the display may activate the touch tracking function (Touch Tracking).

The Playback screen

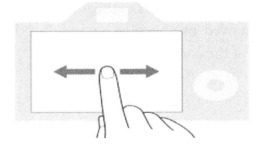

In the course of single-image playbacks, the screen should be swiped rightwards or leftwards to go to the next or previous image.

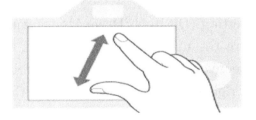

During single-image playbacks, the displayed image may be shrunk or expanded by bringing two fingers together or moving them apart on the screen (pinch-in / pinch-out).

- Double-tapping the display magnifies a still picture or closes the enlarged view.
- Touch actions may be used to stop and resume playback of a movie.

Use control wheel

On the screen shown when the Fn button is hit or the menu screen, the selection frame may be moved by touching or rotating the right/left/bottom/top portion of the control wheel.

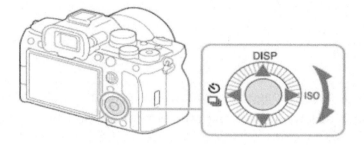

- The functions Display Setting (DISP), / (Drive Mode), and ISO (ISO) are assigned to the upper/left/right portions of the control wheel, respectively. In addition, some duties may be assigned to the right/left/bottom portion and the center of the control wheel, as well as to its rotation.
- You may display the previous/next picture during playbacks by tapping the left/right portion of the control wheel or by spinning the wheel.

Use the multiple-select box

The focus area is movable by dragging the multi-selector to the right, left, down, or up. Additionally, you may specify functions to be activated when the center of the multiselector is pushed.

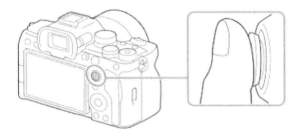

- Place your finger exactly above the multi-selector to operate it with more precision.
- The focus area can be moved whenever [Focus Area] is put at the parameters below:

  ➤ [Zone]
  ➤ [Spot: S] / [Spot: M] / [Spot: L]
  ➤ [Expand Spot]
  ➤ [Tracking: Zone]
  ➤ [Tracking: Spot S] / [Tracking: Spot M] / [Tracking: Spot L]
  ➤ [Tracking: Expand Spot]

- The [Focus Standard] Fn is designated to the middle of the multi-selector under default settings.

Use mode dial and Movie/S&Q/Still dial

The Movie/S&Q/Still dial as well as the mode dial can be used to choose a shooting mode in accordance with the purpose of the shoot and the subject.

Movie/S&Q/Still dial

The Movie/S&Q/Still dial can be used to choose a shooting mode.

The Movie/S&Q/Still dial should be turned while the lock release button at the front of the Movie/S&Q/Still dial is pressed.

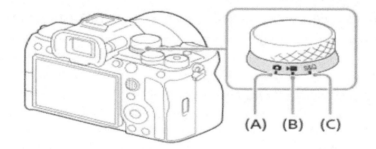

(A) The Still image shoot mode

(B) The Movie record mode

(C) The Slow-mo/quick-mo shoot mode

Hint

- The menu items displayed differ based on the position of the Movie/S&Q/Still dial.

Mode dial

Exposure mode selected ascertains how the F value (aperture) as well as shutter speed is modified.

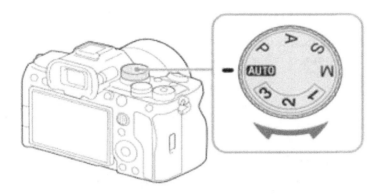

Mode dial	Exposure mode	Description
AUTO (Auto)	Intelligent Auto	The camera shoots with automatic scene recognition.
P	Program Auto	Allows you to shoot with the exposure adjusted automatically (both the shutter speed and the aperture value). You can set shooting functions such as [📷 ISO].
A	Aperture Priority	The aperture value is given priority and the shutter speed is adjusted automatically. Select this when you want to blur the background or focus on the entire screen.
S	Shutter Priority	The shutter speed is given priority and the aperture value is adjusted automatically. Select this when you want to shoot a fast-moving subject without blurring, or when you want to shoot a water or light trail.

M	Manual Exposure	Manually adjust both the aperture value and shutter speed. You can shoot with your favorite exposure.
1 / 2 / 3	**MR** Recall Camera Setting	You can call up frequently used modes and numerical value settings that have been registered* in advance then shoot the images. *In [**MR** Camera Set. Memory], you can register various shooting settings, such as the exposure mode (P/A/S/M), aperture (F value), and shutter speed.

The method for adjusting exposure in video recording modes depends on the configuration for MENU (Shooting) [Shooting Mode] [Exposure Ctrl Type].

When [Exposure Ctrl Type] is set to [P/A/S/M Mode], use the mode dial to choose the desired exposure mode.

If [Exposure Ctrl Type] is set to [Flexible Exposure Mode], then:

Using the following functions assigned to custom buttons, the ISO sensitivity, shutter speed, and aperture value may be toggled between manual and automated modes.

- Aperture value
  [Auto Manual Switch Settings] > [Av Auto/Manual Switch]
- Shutter speed
  [Auto/Manual Switch Settings] > [Tv Auto/Manual Switch]
- ISO Sensitivity
  [Auto/Manual Switch Settings] > [ISO Auto/Manual Settings]

If the manual setting is chosen, pick the desired value by rotating the rear dial L, the control wheel, or the front dial.

Utilizing the MENU button

The menu screen is shown when the MENU button is pressed. From the menu screen, you may adjust the settings associated with all camera activities, including playback and shooting, or perform functions.

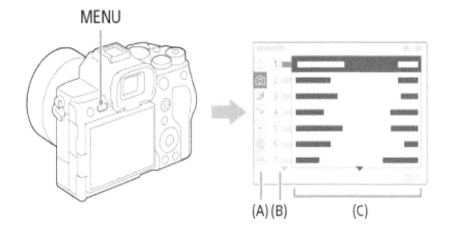

(A)Menu tab: These are grouped by usage scenario, like network settings, playback, shooting, etc.

(B) The Menu group: Every tab menu items are categorized by function. The serial number on the tab is the number designated to the group. Check that number to ascertain the placement of the group in use.

(C)The Menu item: Choose the function to be set or executed.

Hint

- The name of the group or tab selected is shown at the screen top.

- Whenever [Touch Operation] is put at [On], touch operations are possible on the menu screen.

The menu screen basics

1. Touch the MENU button to show the menu screen.

2. Navigate within the menu tree and locate the needed menu item by touching the right/left/bottom/top part of the control wheel.

- The menu items displayed vary between the movie recording modes and still image shooting modes.

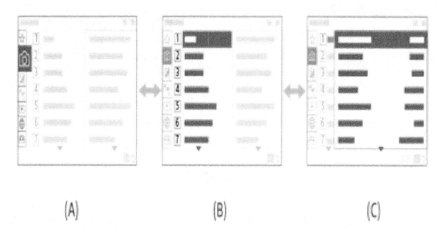

(A)   (B)   (C)

(A) The Menu tabs

(B) The Menu groups

(C) The Menu items

3. Touch the middle of the control wheel to choose the menu item.

The execution or setting screen for the chosen item will show on the monitor.

4. Choose a parameter and/or perform the function.

- If you'd like to cancel altering the parameter, touch the MENU button and return to the former screen.

5. Touch the MENU button to quit the menu screen. You will go back to the playback or shooting screen.

Relationship between the menu screen and Movie/S&Q/Still dial

The menu items and menu groups shown in the [Focus], [Exposure/Color], and [Shooting] tabs differ based on the position of the Movie/S&Q/Still dial.

The menu items and menu groups displayed are the similar in the slow-motion/quick-motion shooting modes as well as the movie recording modes.

Still image shooting modes

The menu items for shooting still images are shown.

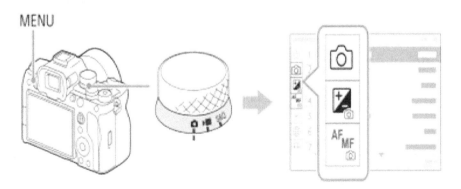

Since movies can be recorded using the Movie (MOVIE) button even under still image shooting mode, certain fundamental movie menu items are also shown.

Slow-mo and quick-mo shooting modes/movie record mode

The menu items needed to record movies are shown.

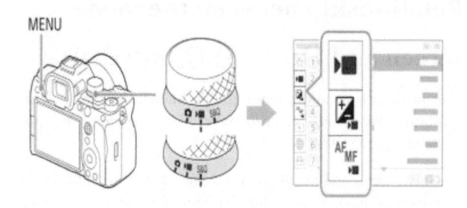

Use the Function (Fn) button

If the function (Fn) button is pressed while shooting, the function menu comprising the functions frequently used like the Focus Mode and Drive Mode is shown on the screen, letting you call the functions up quickly.

Model of function menu

The items displayed vary based on the status of the camera.

Hint

- Launch MENU → 🧰 (The Setup) → [Operations Customize] →[Fn Menu Set.], have your favourite functions registered on the function menu. Twelve functions can be registered shooting still images as well as twelve functions for separately shooting movies.

- Whenever [Touch Operation] is put at [On], touch operations are possible on the menu screen.

- Whenever [Touch Operation] is put at [On], [Fn Menu Settings] can also be opened by holding the icon on the function menu down.

- Whenever **Swipe Up** is assigned to **launch Fn Menu,** you can use touch operations to display the **Function menu** as you swipe your shooting screen up quickly.

- To exit the function menu, you can swipe down from the outside of the Function menu, or better still, you can tap the outside of the function menu.

1. Repeatedly touch the DISP on the control wheel to show a screen mode apart from [For viewfinder].

2. Touch the Function (Fn) button.

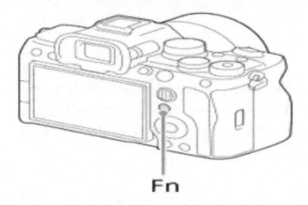

Fn

3. Touch the right/left/bottom/top part of the control wheel to choose the function to be set.

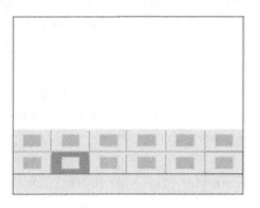

4. Choose the needed setting by turning the front dial and pressing the middle of the control wheel.

Certain functions could be fine-tuned via the rear dial R or rear dial L.

Use the custom (C) buttons

If the functions that are frequently used are assigned to the custom buttons (C1 – C4) in advance, those functions can be quickly called up by touching the button during playback or shooting. By default, suggested functions are designated to the custom buttons.

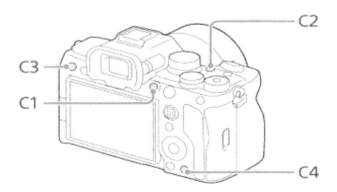

To change/check the functions of custom buttons

The function presently designated to the custom buttons can be confirmed using the procedure below.

Go to MENU → ⊞ (The Setup) → [Operations Customize] → [▢ Dial Setting/Custom Key], [▶◼ Custom Key/Dial Set.] or [▶ Custom Key Setting].

If you'd like to alter the function of a custom button, touch the middle of the control wheel with the custom button selected.

The functions assignable to that button would appear. Choose the desired function.

To utilize the Display Settings button (DISP)

By pressing the Display Setting (DISP) button, it is possible to alter the material shown on the screen during playback and shooting. The display changes whenever the DISP button is pressed. Both the monitor and the viewfinder display may be selected independently.

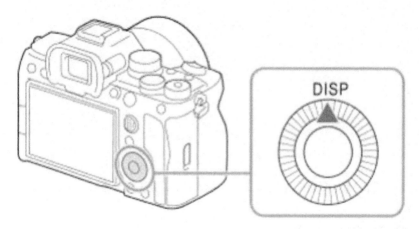

Hint

- The DISP button can be used to power the monitor off. Check mark [Monitor Off] under MENU → 🧰 (Setup) → [Operation Customize] → [DISP (Screen Disp) Set] → [Monitor].

While shooting (The Monitor)

Display All Information→ No Display Information → Histogram → Level → for viewfinder → Display All Info.

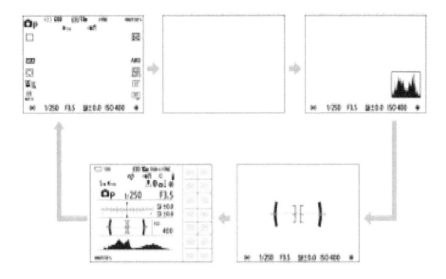

While shooting (Viewfinder)

Choose Level → choose No Display Information → touch on Histogram → touch on Level

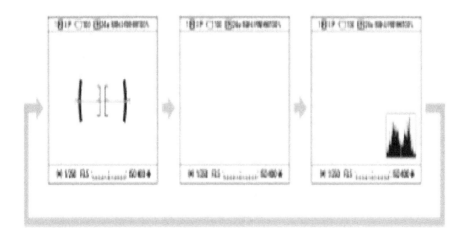

To change the information shown on the viewfinder, touch the DISP button while looking into the viewfinder.

During playback (Viewfinder/Monitor)

Display Info. → Histogram → No Disp. Information. → Display Information.

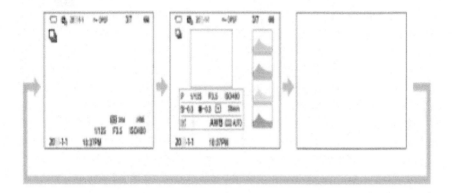

If the picture has an underexposed or overexposed area, the correlating section would blink on the histogram display (underexposed/overexposed warning).

The playback settings are also used in [Auto Review].

Tips

The contents displayed as well as their position displayed in the illustration is simply a guideline, and might vary from the real display.

The following aren't displayed under default settings.

- Monitor Off
- Display All Information. (whenever viewfinder is being used)

[For viewfinder] can't be shown under movie recording modes. Should the monitor display be put at [For viewfinder], the display switches to all info once movie shooting begins.

72

To use the Delete button

A picture currently being shown can be deleted by touching the Delete (🗑) button.

Once a confirmation message appears after touching the button, choose [Delete] using the control wheel and press the center button.

About two or more images may be erased simultaneously.

Choose MENU → (Playback) → [Delete] → [Delete]. After that, choose the images to be erased.

Hint

- Upon configuring MENU (The Playback) By setting [The Delete] [Erase by pressing twice] to [On], photos may be removed by simultaneously pressing the button twice.
- In addition to the single-image playback screen, the Delete button may be used for the following functions:
- With Custom Key
- For In-Camera Guide

Utilizing the AEL button

If the subject is not sufficiently bright when the camera is aimed at it and the shutter button is halfway depressed, the AEL button may be pushed at the required brightness to lock the exposure (AE lock feature) and conduct metering. As soon as exposure is locked, refocus on the subject and shoot the photograph.

AEL

Hint

- Under default settings, [AEL hold] is designated to the AEL button.

Use AF-ON button

In the instances below, the AF-ON button may be used to change the focus without depressing the shutter button halfway ([AF On] function).

- When you need to concentrate at specified shooting distances while anticipating the location of the subject.
- When you must focus and release the shutter independently.

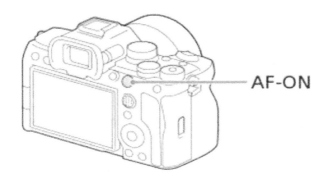

AF-ON

Use rear dial and front dial (R/L)

In the following instances, the two rear dials or the front dial (R/L) may be utilized to rapidly adjust the setting values:

- When changing the shutter speed or aperture value is necessary.
- When you need to adjust the camera's settings while shooting.

During playback, the photos may be navigated by turning the dials.

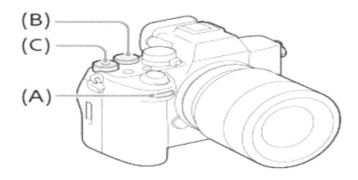

(A): The Front dial

(B): The Rear dial L

(C): The Rear dial R

Hint

The [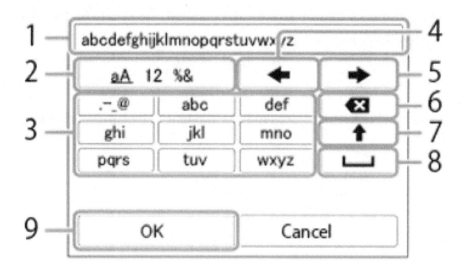 ▶■ Custom Key/Dial Set.]/[◉ Custom Key/Dial Set.] can be used to designate the needed functions to every dial.

You can also use The [My Dial Settings] function can also be used to designate your needed functions to the dials, and those functions recalled when needed.

The keyboard

Whenever manual character entry is needed, a keyboard is shown on the screen.

1. Input panel. The characters entered are shown.

2. Switch character types. Every time this key is pressed, the character type switches between symbols, numerals, and alphabet letters.

3. Keyboard. Every time this key is pressed, the characters correlating with that key would be shown one after the other in

order. To change letters from lowercase to uppercase, touch ↑ (Up arrow).

4. ← (Left arrow). The cursor is moved leftwards in the input box.

5. → (Right arrow). The cursor is moved rightwards in the input box. This key can also be used in finalizing the input of a character that is being edited and go on to the next character.

6. ⊗ (Delete). The character preceding the cursor is deleted.

7. ↑ (Up arrow). Changes a letter to lower or upper case.

8. ⎵ (Space). Inputs a space.

9. OK. Touch this key after inputting characters to finalize the inputted characters.

The system of inputting alphabetic characters is described below.

1. Using the control wheel, navigate the cursor to the needed key.

- Every time the middle of the control wheel is pressed, the characters changes

- To change the letter to lower or upper case, touch ↑ (Up arrow).

2. Once the desired character appears, touch → (Right arrow) to approve the character.

- Ensure that one character is confirmed per time. If a character isn't confirmed, the succeeding character can't be entered.

- Even if the ➡ (Right arrow) is not pressed, the inputted character would be confirmed automatically after many seconds.

3. Once you're done inputting all the characters, finalize the inputted characters by pressing [OK].

- Input can be cancelled by selecting [Cancel].

BATTERY CHARGING

Insert/remove battery pack

1. The battery cover can be opened by sliding the switch on it.

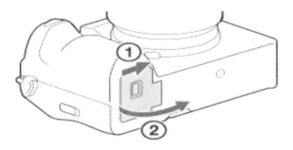

2. Put the battery pack in with the battery's tip pressing the lock lever (A) till the battery is locked into place.

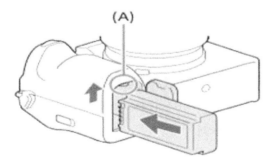

3. Close up the cover and move the switch towards the LOCK side.

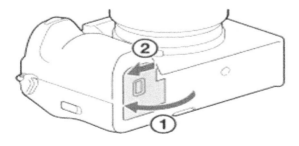

Take out the battery pack

Ensure that the access lamp isn't lit, and switch the camera off. Afterwards, move the lock lever (A) and take the battery pack out. Apply caution so that the battery pack is not dropped.

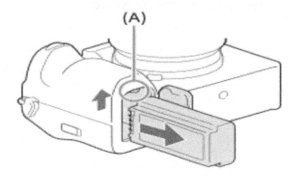

Use Ac Adaptor to power your device battery pack

Turn the camera off.

The camera, with the battery pack inserted, should be connected to the AC Adaptor (provided) via the USB cable, and plug the AC Adaptor to the wall socket (wall outlet).

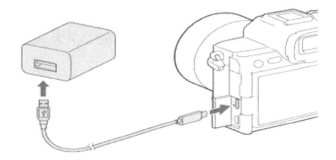

The camera's charge lamp (orange)

If it is Lit: it means it is charging

If it is Off: It means the charging is completed

If it is Flashing: It means it is either charging, but temporarily paused or charging error as a result of the camera not being within the appropriate temperature range

- Charging time (Fully charge): Charging takes around 255 minutes. The given charging time is applicable when a completely drained battery pack is being charged at 77 °F (25 °C).
- Depending with the circumstances and use conditions, the charging process may take longer. The charge light turns off when charging is complete. If the charge bulb illuminates and then quickly turns off, the battery is fully charged.

Important

- From the Micro/Multi USB connector, USB charging is not available. The USB Type-C port may be utilized to charge the battery pack. When use the Battery Charger/AC Adapter, a nearby wall socket (wall outlet) should be utilized. In the event of a problem, unscrew the plug from the wall socket (wall outlet) to disconnect it from the power source. If the product is used in conjunction with the charge light, be aware that the camera is still connected to the power source even when the lamp has turned off.

- If you turned on the camera, it would get electricity from the wall socket (wall outlet), allowing you to operate it. However, the battery pack will not be charged.

Utilize a USB-standard or USB cable (provided).

Using a mobile battery or commercially available AC adaptors to charge the battery.

A USB cable may be used to charge from external power sources, such as a mobile battery or USB AC adapters that are commercially available.

Fast charging is available whenever a device that supports USB Power Delivery (USB-PD) is connected to the product.

Connect an external power supply to the camera's USB Type-C port after turning it off.

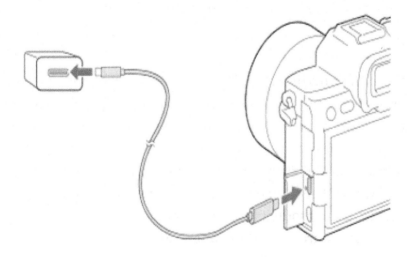

Use your Sony battery charger/AC Adaptor

The battery charger (not included) may be used with the AC Adaptor (included) in any location or nation with a 100-240V, 50/60Hz power supply. Depending on the region/country, a plug adapter may be necessary to connect to the wall socket (wall outlet). Consult a travel agent, etc., and bring one with you ahead.

Do not use electronic voltage transformers, since doing so may cause a problem.

Power from a wall socket (wall outlet)

Utilize the included AC adaptor to playback and capture photographs while the wall outlet provides power (wall outlet). This maintains the battery power of the product. By adding a USB Power Delivery (USB-PD)-compatible device to the camera, the battery usage might be decreased even more.

1. Insert a fully charged battery pack into the device.

- The camera will not operate if there is no remaining battery power. Insert a battery pack that is adequately charged into the camera.

2. The USB cable should be connected to the product's USB Type-C port.

3. Plug the AC adapter into the wall socket (wall outlet) (provided).

4. Turn the camera On.

- The symbol ( ) showing that USB power is being provided will show on the monitor, and power supply will begin.

Note

1. USB power cannot be delivered Via the Micro/Multi USB Terminal. Provide electricity via the USB Type-C port.

2. Since the power is on, the battery pack will not be charged even if the AC Adaptor is connected to the product.

3. Under some settings, the battery pack may provide supplemental power even while the AC adapter is in use.

3. Do not remove the battery pack while the wall socket is supplying electricity (wall outlet). When the battery pack is removed, the product is switched off.

4. The USB cable should only be attached to or detached from the product while it is shut off.

5. Depending on the temperature of the battery and the camera, the continuous recording period may be decreased when the device is receiving power from the wall outlet (wall outlet).

6. Ensure that a mobile charger is completely charged before to usage whenever it will be utilized as a power source. In addition, be aware of the remaining power on the mobile charger while it is in use.

7. It is impossible to guarantee operation with all external power suppliers.

Inset or remove my memory card

SD memory cards and CFexpress Type A memory cards can be used with this product.

1. Open the memory card cover by sliding the switch on it.

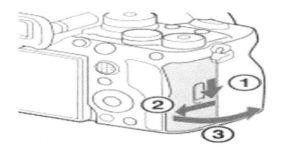

2. Position your card into the camera slot 1.

- When using two memory cards, place the second card in slot 2.
- Slot 1 & 2 are compatible with SD mcards and CFexpress Type A cards.
- By default, photographs are saved to the memory card placed in Slot 1.
- Insert the CFexpress Type A memory card with the label facing the display, and the SD memory card with the terminal facing the monitor. Insert until it snaps into position.

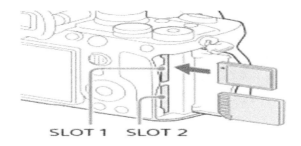

SLOT 1   SLOT 2

3. Close up the cover.

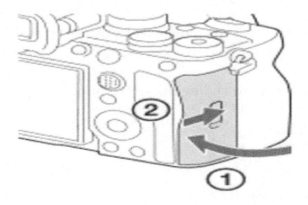

Hint

- When using a memory card for the first time with the device, it is advised that the card be formatted on the camera for improved performance stability.
- The recording memory card slot may be changed by entering the MENU and selecting Shooting > Media > Record Media Settings > Recording Media or Recording Media.

Slot 1 is utilised under normal settings.

To record one image concurrently on both memory cards or to organize recorded images on both memory card slots according on image type (movie/still image), open the MENU, go to Shooting > Media > Record Media Settings, and then change the Recording Media settings or press Recording Media.

Remove your memory card

Remove the memory card cover and ensure that the access lamp (A) is off, afterwards remove the memory card by lightly pushing it in once.

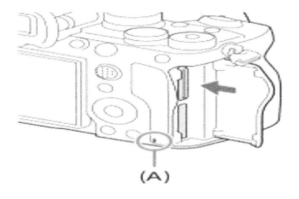

(A)

Attach or remove lens

Turn off the camera before installing or withdrawing the lens.

1. Remove the body cap (A) from the product and the rear lens cap (B) from the back of the lens.

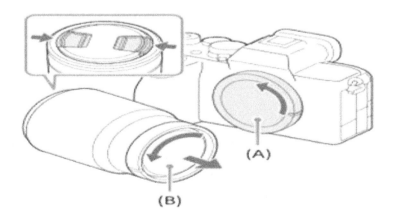

It is advised that you replace the front lens cover after shooting.

2. Align the mounting indexes (two white index markings) on the camera and lens to attach the lens.

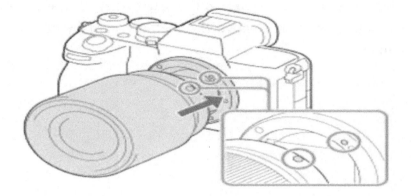

To prevent debris and dust from entering the camera, hold the product with the lens mount facing downwards.

3. While gently pushing the lens towards the product, steadily slide the lens in the direction of the arrow until it locks into place.

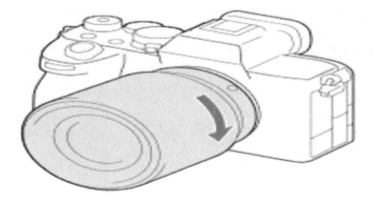

Ensure that the lens is kept straight throughout the attachment process.

While pressing the lens release button (A), move the lens in the direction of the arrow until it stops. Connect the body cap to the product and the rear and front lens caps to the lens to prevent dirt and dust from entering the lens and camera after the lens has been removed.

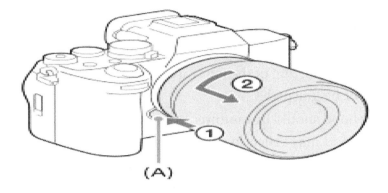

(A)

The Lens hood

We recommend using the lens hood to prevent light from beyond the frame from affecting the picture. The lens hood must be installed such that the lens and lens hood indexes are aligned. (Some lenses may lack a lens hood index).

Important

- When removing or attaching the lens, it should be done swiftly and in a dust-free environment.
- Do not press the lens release button during lens attachment.
- Do not use force while attaching the lens.
- The A-mount lens requires a Mount Adaptor (not supplied) in order to function (not included). Check the Mount Adaptor's included operation handbook before using the Mount Adaptor.
- Full-frame photography requires lenses that are compatible with the full-frame format.

- When using a lens with a tripod socket, it is necessary to connect a tripod to the lens' tripod socket in order to counterbalance the lens' weight.
- When carrying a camera with an attached lens, both the lens and camera should be gripped securely.
- The extended portion of the lens for adjusting focus or zoom should not be grasped.
- The lens hood should be mounted appropriately. Otherwise, the lens hood may reflect partially on the image or have no impact.
- The lens hood should be removed whenever the flash is being used as the hood obstructs the flash light and might show as a shadow on the picture.

SETTING THE CAMERA TIME, DATE, AND LANGUAGE

When the camera is switched on for the first time, the product is initialized, or the internal rechargeable backup battery is drained, the screen for setting the time, date, and language is shown automatically.

1. To turn the camera on, move the Power (ON/OFF) switch to the "ON" position.

2. Select the desired language and then press the center of the control wheel.

3. Ensure that [Enter] is selected on the screen for the confirmation of location/date/time, and then touch the control wheel's center.

4. Select the required geographic location, select [Daylight Savings Time], and then tap the center.

The bottom/top of the control wheel may be used to activate/deactivate Daylight Savings Time.

5. Select the date format (day/month/year) and press the center button.

6. Adjust the time and date (hour/minute/second) and then tap the center.

To choose the geographic area, time, or date again at a later time, select MENU (Setup) Location. [Location/Date] [Location/Date/Time Setting].

To preserve time and date

This gadget contains an inbuilt rechargeable battery that retains the time, date, and other settings regardless of whether it is switched on or off, or whether the battery pack is drained or charged.

The inbuilt rechargeable backup battery may be charged by putting a fully charged battery pack into the device and keeping the camera off for at least twenty-four hours.

If the clock is reset every time the pack is recharged, the inbuilt rechargeable backup battery may get depleted. Contact your servicing facility for further information.

Hint

- By connecting a smartphone and the camera through the Bluetooth function, the camera can be operated via the smartphone and images transferred from the product to the smartphone. A smartphone can be connected to the product by setting the time and date, and afterwards following the instructions on the screen to carry out pairing.

Tips

- If the time and date setting is annulled halfway, the screen for setting the time and date shows each time the camera is turned on.
- The camera's inbuilt clock might display time errors. The time should be adjusted at steady intervals.

CONFIRMATIONS PRIOR TO SHOOTING

In this part, you will be introduced to the features and settings of the camera that you should be aware of while using it. We recommend confirming these functionalities and settings before utilizing the product.

Capture still photos (The Intelligent Auto)

This section describes how [Intelligent Auto] still photos may be captured. Under the [Intelligent Auto] mode, the device automatically focuses and determines the exposure based on the shooting circumstances.

1. Rotate the Movie/S&Q/Still dial to (Still) to choose the still picture mode.

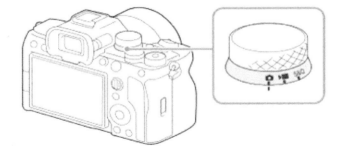

The Movie/S&Q/Still dial should be turned while touching the lock release button at its front.

2. Put the mode dial to **AUTO** (Auto Mode).

- This sets the shooting mode set to **i◌** (Intelligent Auto).

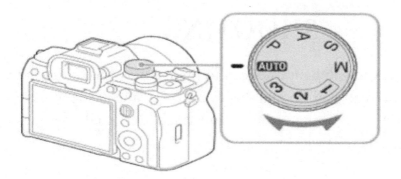

- Rotate its mode dial as you're pressing mode dial lock releasing button at the middle of the mode dial.

3. Adjust the monitor's viewing angle while holding the product. Or glance through the product's viewfinder while holding it.

4. Whenever a zoom lens is attached, images may be magnified by rotating the zoom ring.

5. Adjust the focus by pressing the shutter button halfway.

The indication illuminates and a beep is heard when the image is in focus.

6. Press the shutter button all the way down.

To manually choose the focus mode (Focus Area/ Focus Mode).

Indicating a focus mode, such as selecting Single-shot AF () for still objects or landscapes and Continuous AF () for mobile subjects, makes it considerably simpler to concentrate on a specific topic. The range and location of the focal point may also be set through [Focus Area].

To photograph with the eyes as the focal point

Under [Face/Eye AF], the [Face/Eye Prior. in AF] function is active by default; hence, the Eye AF function may be utilized instantly.

Taking photographs with the focus focused on a certain topic (Focus-lock)

When focusing on a subject, the shutter button is depressed halfway while the focus is locked. Change to the desired composition and depress the shutter button completely to take the photograph.

Stationary subjects may be locked in sharp focus. Toggle [Focus Mode] on (Single-shot AF).

Setting [Focus Area] to [Center Fix] facilitates concentration on subjects in the center of the screen.

Hint

- When the camera is unable to focus automatically, the focus indicator flashes while the beep is silent. Either the focus setting should be adjusted or the photo should be retaken.

  In [Continuous AF] mode, the focus indicator (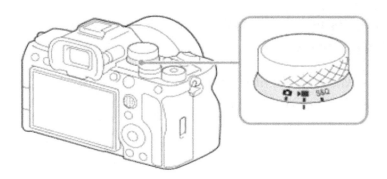) illuminates, but there is no beep to indicate that focus has been achieved.

Tips

- After firing, a sign indicating that data is being written is shown. This sign indicates that the memory card should not be removed while it is shown. This will prevent photographs from being captured normally.

Shoot movies (Intelligent Auto)

This section describes how movies may be recorded utilizing the [Intelligent Auto] mode. Under the [Intelligent Auto] mode, the device automatically focuses and determines the exposure based on the recording circumstances.

1. To choose movie recording mode, turn the Movie/S&Q/Still dial to (Movie).

The Movie/S&Q/Still dial should be turned while touching the lock release button at its front.

2. Put the mode dial to Auto Mode (**AUTO**).

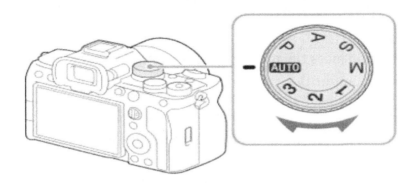

3. Begin recording by pressing the Movie (MOVIE) button.

MOVIE

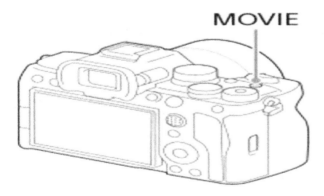

4. Touch the MOVIE button a second time to end recording.

Selecting record File Format

Depending on the recording format (XAVC S-I HD/XAVC S-I 4K/XAVC S HD/XAVC S 4K/XAVC HS 4K), the compatibility and resolution vary. Determine the format based on the purpose of the film being shot.

Choosing the picture resolution or frame rate (Movie Settings)

The frame rate of a movie determines the fluidity of motion. ([Movie Settings] -> [Rec Frame Rate])

The bit rate influences the image's quality. ([Movie Configuration] [Record Configuration])

When the bit-rate is high, the amount of data rises, allowing for the production of high-quality films. Nonetheless, this would result in increased data quantities.

Choose the bit rate and frame rate based on the intended use and your own choice.

Exposure adjustment (Exposure Mode/Exposure Ctrl Type).

When [Exposure Ctrl Type] is set to [P/A/S/M Mode], the exposure mode is selected using the same aperture setting and shutter speed combination as when shooting a still picture.

When [Exposure Ctrl Type] is set to [Flexible Exposure Mode], ISO sensitivity, aperture value, and shutter speed may be manually or automatically adjusted.

To choose the manner of focusing (Focus Area/Focus Mode).

For [Focus Mode], choose Continuous AF () or Manual Focus (). When [Focus Area] is set, the focus area may be defined. Even while shooting with manual focus, you may temporarily switch to autofocus using the techniques below.

Touch the custom button [AF On] is assigned to, or half-press the shutter button.

Press the key customized for [Eye AF].

Tap the topic on the display.

Four-channel recording of movie sound

Connect a Sony accessory compatible with 24-bit and 4-channel audio recording to the Multi Interface Shoe of the camera.

Hint

- The function to stop/start movie recording may also be set to a key.
- By pressing the shutter button halfway while filming, you may fast focus the camera. (In certain situations, the auto-focus sound may be recorded.)
- While a movie is being shot, the focus area, exposure compensation, and ISO sensitivity settings may be altered.
- While filming, it may be possible to capture the noises of the lens and camera. To prevent the recording of sounds, set [Audio Recording] to [Off].
- To prevent the zoom ring's operation sound from being captured while using a power zoom lens, we recommend

recording videos using the lens' zoom lever. When adjusting the zoom lever of the lens, use care so as not to flip the lever.

Note

- After shooting, a sign indicating that data is being written is shown. The memory card should not be removed while the corresponding icon is shown.
- Movies cannot be recorded while data is being written. Wait until data writing is complete and "STBY" is shown before to capturing the video.
- If the Overheating warning icon appears, the camera's temperature has increased. Turn off the camera, allow it to cool, and wait until it is ready to be used again.
- During continuous filming, the temperature of the camera tends to rise, and you may sense that it is warm. There is no malfunction here. Moreover, [internal temperature is high. [Allow it to cool] may manifest. In such cases, switch off the power and allow the product to cool before commencing photography.
- Once a movie is recorded, you may record another movie by pressing the MOVIE button again. Depending on the temperature of the battery or the device, recording may cease to safeguard the product.

SHOOTING FUNCTION

Choose a shooting mode

Intelligent Auto

The camera utilizes automated scene recognition.

1. Set the Movie/S&Q/still mode using the Movie/S&Q/still mode dial.

2. Place the mode dial in Auto.

- This function sets the mode to [Intelligent Auto].

3. Direct the product towards the subject.

- As soon as the product detects the scene, the corresponding icon appears on the screen.

4. Adjust focus and shoot the picture.

Scene Recognition

This function lets the camera automatically identify shooting conditions.

Note

- The camera won't identify a scene when images are shot using zoom functions instead of optical zoom.
- The product might not properly identify the scenes under specific shooting conditions.
- Under [Intelligent Auto] mode, almost all the functions are fixed automatically, and you can't adjust the settings yourself.

Program Auto

Permits taking photographs with the exposure automatically adjusted (both the aperture value and the shutter speed).

Shooting functions such as [ISO] can be set.

1. Set the Movie/S&Q/ Still mode dial to the desired mode.

2. Select P on the mode dial (Program Auto).

3. Adjust the camera's shooting features to your specifications.

4. Adjust the focal point and capture the subject.

Program Shift (specific to still image shooting)

When the flash is not being used, the aperture (F-value) and shutter speed combination can be changed without affecting the product's predetermined exposure. when the flash is not being used, the aperture (F-value) and shutter speed combination can be changed without affecting the product's predetermined exposure.

Rotate the rear dial L/front dial to choose the desired combination of shutter speed and aperture setting.

On the display, "P" becomes "P*" anytime the rear dial L/front dial is rotated.

Program shift may be cancelled by selecting a mode other than [Program Auto] or by turning off the camera.

Note

Depending on the ambient brightness, the program shift may not be implemented.

Change the shooting mode to anything other than "P" or turn the power off to cancel the setting.

Whenever there is a change in brightness, the shutter speed and aperture (F-value) both vary, although the amount of shift remains constant.

The Aperture Priority

To shoot, adjust the aperture and modify the range under focus, or defocus the background.

1. Put the Movie/S&Q/Still dial to the needed shooting mode.

2. Put the mode dial to A (Aperture Priority).

3. Choose the needed value by moving the rear dial L/front dial.

- Smaller F-value: The subject stays in focus, while the objects beyond and in front of it are blurred. Larger F-value: The subject, its background and foreground and are all in focus.
- If the aperture value set happens to be unsuitable for proper exposure, the shutter speed on the screen for shooting blinks. If this occurs, the aperture value should be changed.

4. Modify the focus and capture the subject.

- Shutter speed is adjusted automatically to get proper exposure.

Note

- The image brightness on the screen might vary from the real picture being shot.

Shutter Priority

The movement of a mobile subject can be expressed in different ways by altering the shutter speed, for instance, at the point of moving using high speed shutter, or as a trailing picture with low speed shutter.

1. Put the Movie/S&Q/Still dial to the needed shooting mode.

2. Put the mode dial to S (Shutter Priority).

3. Choose the needed value by moving the rear dial L/front dial.

- If appropriate exposure can't be gotten after set-up, the aperture value on the screen for shooting will blink. If this occurs, alter the shutter speed.

4. Adjust focus and capture the shot.

- The aperture is adjusted automatically to get proper exposure.

Hint

- To stop the product from shaking when a slow shutter speed is selected, a tripod stand should be used.
- When indoor sports scenes are shot, ISO sensitivity should be set to a higher value.

Note

- The SteadyShot warning indicator doesn't show in shutter speed priority mode.
- Whenever [Long Exposure NR] is put to [On] and shutter speed is 1 second(s) or more with a [Shutter Type] apart from [Electronic Shutter] is fixed, noise reduction after

shooting is carried out for the same duration that the shutter was open. Nevertheless, shots can no longer be taken once noise reduction is in progress.

The brightness of the picture on the screen might vary from the real picture being shot.

Manual Exposure

Shots can be taken with the specific exposure setting by altering both the aperture and shutter speed.

1. Set the Movie/S&Q/Still dial to the specific shooting mode.

2. Put the mode dial to M (Manual Exposure).

3. Choose the specific aperture value by moving the front dial.

Choose the specific shutter speed by moving the rear dial L.

- You can choose which dial alters the shutter speed and aperture value using [▶️ Custom Key/Dial Set.] or [📷 Custom Key/Dial Set.].

- [📷 ISO] can also be set to [ISO AUTO] under manual exposure mode. ISO value changes automatically to attain the suitable exposure with the shutter speed and aperture value set.

- Whenever [📷 ISO] is put to [ISO AUTO], the ISO value indicator blinks whenever the value set is unsuitable for proper exposure. Should this happen, either the aperture value or the shutter speed should be changed.

- Whenever [📷 ISO] is put to apart from [ISO AUTO], Metered Manual ("M.M.")* should be used to check the exposure value.

106

| Toward | +: | Pictures | become | brighter. |
| Toward | -: | Pictures | become | darker. |

o: Suitable exposure analysed by the product.

4. Indicates over/under for proper exposure. It is shown through the use of numerical values on the monitor as well as with the metering indicator on the viewfinder.

Alter the focus and capture the shot.

Hint

- By turning the rear dial L/front dial while pushing the AEL button, the aperture (F-value) and shutter speed combination can be changed without changing the exposure value set. (Manual shift)

Note

- The Metered Manual indicator doesn't show whenever [ISO] is put to [ISO AUTO].
- Whenever the amount of ambient light is greater than the Metered Manual's metering range, the Metered Manual indicator blinks.
- The SteadyShot warning indicator doesn't show under manual exposure mode.
- The brightness of the picture on the screen might vary from the real picture being shot.

Bulb shooting

Trailing images of a subject's movement can be shot using long exposure. Trails from fireworks or stars, etc., are best shot using bulb shooting.

1. Set the Movie/S&Q/ Still dial to ⬛ (Still) to choose the still image shooting mode.

2. Put the mode dial to Manual Exposure (M).

3. Rotate the rear dial L in the clockwise direction till [BULB] is shown.

4. Choose the F-value (aperture value) with the front dial.

5. Partly push the shutter button down to focus.

6. Push and hold the shutter button throughout the shoot.

- Inasmuch as you press the shutter button, the shutter stays open.

Hint

- Whenever fireworks, etc. are being shot, focus should be at infinity under manual focus mode. If a lens with unclear infinity is used, the focus should be adjusted on the fireworks in the part you'd like to focus on beforehand.
- To be able to carry out bulb shooting without bringing about deterioration in the image quality, we suggest that you begin shooting while the product is cool.
- Images have the tendency to get blurred in the course of bulb shooting. It is advised that a tripod, a remote commander fitted with lock function (not included) or a

Bluetooth remote commander (not included) be used. Whenever the Bluetooth remote commander is being used, bulb shooting can be started by pushing the shutter button on the remote commander. To end bulb shooting, push the shutter button on the remote commander a second time. For the second remote commander to be used, a model which can be attached using the Micro/Multi USB terminal should be used.

Note

- The higher the exposure time, the higher the visible noise on the picture.
- Whenever [Long Exposure NR] is put to [On], noise reduction is carried out after shooting for the same length of time that the shutter was open. Shots can't be taken while noise reduction is being undergone.

The Shutter speed can't be set to [BULB] in the situations below:

- Whenever the drive mode is put to the following:
  - [Cont. Shooting]
  - [Self-timer(Continuous)]
  - [Cont. Bracket]
- [Shutter Type] is put to [Electronic Shutter].

If the above functions are used whenever shutter speed is put to [BULB], shutter speed is temporarily put to 30 seconds.

Exposure Control Type

Whenever the mode dial is set to P/A/S/M, the method for choosing the exposure (ISO sensitivity, shutter speed, and aperture) can be selected while shooting movies. Using [P/A/S/M Mode], the exposure mode can be selected via P/A/S/M on the mode dial. Via [Flexible Exp. Mode], you can singularly alternate between the manual and automatic settings for shutter speed, ISO sensitivity, and aperture value similar to the exposure control system of professional cameras.

1. MENU → ▶■■ (Shooting) → [Shooting Mode] → [Exposure Ctrl Type] → desired setting.

Menu Options

- **P/A/S/M Mode:** Choose the specific exposure mode from among [Manual Exposure], [Shutter Priority], [Aperture Priority], and [Program Auto].
- **Flexible Exp. Mode:** Sets the ISO sensitivity, shutter speed, and aperture value manually (Manual) or automatically (Auto). You can alternate between the manual and automatic settings via the designated custom key, or change the ISO sensitivity, shutter speed, and aperture values by rotating the rear dial L, rear dial R, front dial and control wheel.

Note

- Even when [Exposure Ctrl Type] is put to [Flexible Exp. Mode], whenever movies are shot by pushing the movie (MOVIE) button in still image shooting mode, the movie would be shot in the exposure mode chosen using the mode dial.

Auto/Manual Switch Setting

Whenever movies are shot, you can individually alternate between the manual and automatic settings for ISO sensitivity, shutter speed, and aperture as is done with the exposure control system of professional cameras. Put [Exposure Ctrl Type] to [Flexible Exp. Mode] in advance.

1. Go to MENU → [±] (Exposure/Color) → [Exposure] → [Auto/Manual Swt. Set.] → desired setting item.

Menu options

- **Av Automatic/Manual Switch:** Alternates aperture value between [Manual] and [Auto].
- **Tv Automatic/Manual Switch:** Alternates shutter speed between [Manual] and [Auto].
- **ISO Automatic/Manual Setting:** Alternates ISO sensitivity between [Manual] and [Auto].

Alternate between Manual and Automatic using custom keys

Whenever [Exposure Ctrl Type] is put to [Flexible Exp. Mode], the below functions are designated to the custom keys while recording movies.

- [Av Automatic/Manual Swt]: Custom 2 (C2) button
- [Tv Automatic/Manual Swt]: C4 button
- [ISO Automatic/Manual Set]: C1 button

111

Every time the corresponding custom key is pressed, the ISO sensitivity, shutter speed, or aperture value alternates between [Manual] and [Auto]. Whenever [Auto] is chosen, the appropriate exposure is automatically set, and whenever [Manual] is chosen, the ISO sensitivity, shutter speed, and aperture value can be set using the dials below.

- Aperture value: the front dial
- The Shutter speed: the control wheel
- ISO sensor: rear dial L

Note

- Whenever the aperture value is set using the lens aperture ring, the value of the aperture ring takes precedence over the value of the dial.

Automatic Slow Shutter

Sets whether the shutter speed is to be adjusted automatically or not when movies are being recorded if the subject happens to be dark. This function can't be used in the course of slow/quick motion shooting.

1. Launch the MENU → ⊞ (Exposure/Color) → [Exposure] → [Auto Slow Shutter] → desired setting.

Menu options

- On: Makes use of Auto Slow Shutter. Shutter speed slows automatically whenever recording is done in dark places. Noise can be reduced in that movie through the use of slow shutter speed whenever recording is done in a dark location.

112

- Off: Doesn't use Auto Slow Shutter. The movie recorded would be darker compared to when [On] is chosen, but movies can be recorded with minimal object blur and smoother motion.

Note

[Auto Slow Shutter] doesn't function in the situations below:

- ▶■■S The Shutter Priority
- ▶■■M The Manual Exposure
- Whenever [🎥 ISO] is put to apart from [ISO AUTOMATIC]
- When [Exp Ctrl Type] is set to [Flexible Exposure Mode] and the method for adjusting the shutter speed is set to [Manual]

FOCUSING

Choose the focus method (Focus Mode)

Chooses the focus method to fit the subject's movement.

1. Go to MENU, proceed to **AF**_{**MF**} (Focus) → select [AF/MF] → [🖿 Focus Mode] →choose the desired setting.

Menu options

- **AF-S** Single-shot AF: The camera locks the focus immediately focusing is completed. This should be used whenever the subject is stationary.

- **AF-A** Automatic AF: [Continuous AF] and [Single-shot AF] are alternated in accordance to the subject's movement. Whenever the shutter button is partly pressed down, the camera locks the focus once it ascertains that the subject is stationary, or keeps focusing whenever the subject moves. In continuous shooting, the camera automatically shoots using [Continuous AF] after the first shot.

- **AF-C** Continuous AF: The camera keeps focusing while the shutter button is partly pressed and partly held down. This should be used whenever the subject is moving. Under [Continuous AF] mode, there isn't a beep once the product focuses.

- **DMF** DMF: Fine adjustments can be manually made after carrying out auto-focusing, allowing you to focus more quickly on a subject compared to when [Manual Focus] is used right from the start. This is ideal in situations like macro shooting.
- **MF** **Manual Focus:** The focus is manually adjusted. If you can't focus on the specific subject via auto focus, utilise [Manual Focus].

Focus indicator

● (lit):
The main subject is in focus and the focus is locked.

● (flashing):
The subject isn't in focus.

 (lit):
The subject is in focus. The focus would be continuously adjusted in accordance with the subject's movements.

(( )) (Lit):
Focusing is going on progress.

Subjects with whom the use of auto focus is difficult

- Subjects that are distant and dark
- Subjects having poor contrast
- Subjects visible through glass
- Subjects that are moving fast
- Shiny surfaces or reflective light
- Flashing light
- Subjects that are back-lit
- Patterns that are continuously repetitive, like a building's facades
- Subjects within the focusing region with varying focal distances

Hint

- Under [Continuous AF] mode, the focus can be locked by pushing and holding the button that has been designated the [Focus Hold] function.
- Whenever focus is set to infinity under [DMF] mode or [Manual Focus] mode, ensure that the subject being focused on is sufficiently distant by looking through the viewfinder or monitor.

Note

- [Automatic AF] is only available when the lens being used is compatible with phase detection AF.
- When [Automatic AF] or [Continuous AF] is set, the viewing angle might change bit by bit while focusing. This doesn't impact the real recorded images.

- Only [Manual Focus] and [Cont. AF] are available whenever movies are shot or Movie/S&Q/ Still dial is put to ▶️■ (Movie) or S&Q Motion (S&Q).

Select the focus area (Focus Area)

Set the kind of focusing frame whenever auto focus is used in shooting. Choose the mode in accordance with the subject.

1. Launch MENU → go to ^{AF}MF (Focus) → The [Focus Area] → [🖼 Focus Area] → select the needed setting.

Menu options

- [:] Wide: Automatically focuses on the subject occupying the entire screen range. Whenever the shutter button is partly pressed down under still image shooting mode, a green frame is shown around the area under focus.

- ⊔⊔⊔ Zone: On the monitor, choose the zone to be focused on, and the camera automatically selects a focus area.

- [ ] Center Fix: Automatically focuses on the subject in the middle of the image. Create the desired composition by using this alongside the focus-lock function.

- ▣M Spot: S/Spot: M/Spot: L: Allows the focusing frame to be moved to the desired part on the screen as well as to focus on a really small subject in a narrow region.

- ▣ Expand Spot: If the camera can't focus on an individually selected point, it makes use of focus points near the [Spot] as the secondary priority region for focusing.

- [⊡]ː [⊡]ː [⊡]ː [⊡]Mː [⊡]ː **Tracking:** This setting is only available when [📷 Focus Mode] is put to [Continuous AF]. Whenever the shutter button is pushed and held partly down, the camera monitors the subject inside the chosen autofocus area. Direct the cursor at [Tracking] on the setting screen for [📷 Focus Area], and afterwards choose the needed area to begin tracking via the right/left sides of the control wheel. The tracking start region can also be moved to the needed point by assigning the region as a [Tracking: Spot L]/ [Tracking: Spot M]/ [Tracking: Spot S], [Tracking: Zone], or [Tracking: Expand Spot].

Hint

- Under default settings, [📷 Focus Area] is designated to the C2 button.

Note

[📷 Focus Area] is locked at [Wide] in the situations below:

- [Intelligent Auto]

The focus area might not come on whenever the shutter button is completely pressed down at once or in the course of continuous shooting.

When the Movie/S&Q/Still dial is put to ▶️ (Movie) or S&Q Motion (S&Q) or while shooting a movie, [Tracking] can't be chosen for [📷 Focus Area].

Examples of focusing frame display

The focusing frame varies as follows.

When a larger area is being focused on

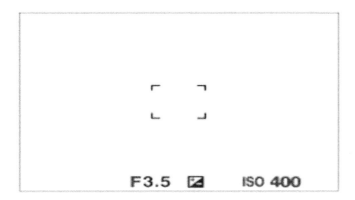

When a smaller area is being focused on

Whenever [📷 Focus Area] is put to [Zone] or [Wide] the focusing frame might alternate between "When focusing on a smaller area" and "When focusing on a larger area" contingent on the situation or subject.

Whenever an A-mount lens with a Mount Adaptor (LA-EA5 or LA-EA3) (not included) is attached, the focusing frame for "When focusing on a smaller area" might be shown. When focus is automatically achieved on the basis of the monitor's entire range

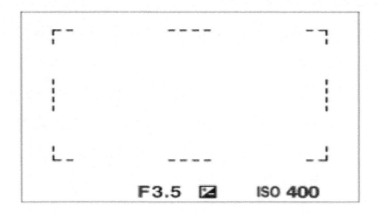

When a zoom function apart from optical zoom is used, the setting for [📷 Focus Area] is deactivated and the focusing frame is displayed by the dotted line. The AF functions with priority around and on the middle area.

Moving the focus area

The focus area can be moved by operating the multi-selector whenever [📷 Focus Area] is put to the parameters below:

- [Zone]
- [Spot: S]/[Spot: M]/[Spot: L]
- [Expand Spot]
- [Tracking: Zone]
- [Tracking: Spot L]/ [Tracking: Spot M]/[Tracking: Spot S]
- [Tracking: Expand Spot]

If [Focus Standard] is assigned to the middle of the multi-selector in advance, the focusing frame can be returned to the subject being tracked or the middle of the monitor by pushing the middle of the multi-selector.

Hint

- Whenever [📷 Focus Area] is put to [Expand Spot] or [Spot], the focusing frame can be moved over a larger distance per time using the multi-selector by putting [📷 AF Frame Move Amt] to [Large].
- The focusing frame can be quickly moved by tapping and pulling it on the monitor. Put [Touch Operation] to [On], and put [Touch Func. in Shooting] to [Touch Focus] in advance.

Temporarily track a object when shooting still images (Tracking On)

- The setting for [📷 Focus Area] to [Tracking] can be temporarily changed while the custom key to which [Tracking On] has been assigned to beforehand is pressed and held down. The setting for [📷 Focus Area] prior to activating [Tracking On] will change to the corresponding [Tracking] setting.

For instance:

[📷 Focus Area] before you activate [Tracking On]	[📷 Focus Area] while [Tracking On] is active
[Wide]	[Tracking: Wide]
[Spot: S]	[Tracking: Spot S]
[Expand Spot]	[Tracking: Expand Spot]

121

Phase detection AF

When phase detection AF points exist within the auto focus region, the camera makes use of the combined autofocus of the contrast AF and phase detection AF.

Note

Phase detection AF is only available when a supported lens is connected. If a lens that's incompatible with phase detection AF is used, the below functions can't be used.

- [Automatic AF]
- [AF Tracking Sensitivity]
- [AF Subj. Shift Sensitivity]
- [AF Transition Speed]

Additionally, even though an applicable lens that was previously bought is used, the phase detection AF may not work unless the lens is updated.

Track the subject (Tracking function)

This product has the function of tracking which tracks the subject, and continues marking them using the focusing frame. The start position can be set to track by choosing from focusing areas, or by indicating via touch operation. The needed function differs contingent on the setting method.

Set the start position to track by focusing area ([Tracking] under Focus Area]

The chosen focusing frame is put as the start point to track, and the tracking begins by pushing the shutter button partly down.

- This function is obtainable under still image shooting mode.
- This function is obtainable whenever [Focus Mode] is put to [Continuous AF].

Set the start position to track through touch operation ([Touch Tracking] under [Touch Function in Shooting])

The subject can be set to track by tapping it on the monitor.

- This function is obtainable under movie shooting mode and still image shooting mode.
- This function is obtainable whenever [Focus Mode] is put to [DMF], [Continuous AF], [Automatic AF], or [Single-shot AF].

Temporarily change the setting for [Focus Area] to [Tracking] ([Tracking On] under [Custom Key/Dial Set.])

Though [📷 Focus Area] is put to apart from [Tracking], the setting for [📷 Focus Area] can be temporarily changed to [Tracking] while pushing and holding the button to which [Tracking On] function is assigned.

- Designate the [Tracking On] function to a specific key via [📷 Custom Key/Dial Set.] beforehand.
- This function is obtainable under still image shooting mode.
- This function is obtainable whenever [📷 Focus Mode] is put to [Continuous AF].

Temporarily pause the tracking function

By touching the button to which [Tracking-Off Toggle] or [Tracking-Off Hold] via [📷 Custom Key/Dial Set.] is assigned, the tracking function can be temporarily paused. Use this function should be used whenever you're in a shooting situation where tracking is starting to get difficult, or whenever the tracking frame changes to a different subject.

If you touch the key to which [Tracking/Face-Off Toggle.] or [Tracking/Face-Off Hold] using [📷 Custom Key/Dial Set.] is assigned, [📷 Face/Eye Prior. in AF] temporarily switches to [Off], discontinuing the tracking function that gives priority to the eyes/face.

This function should be used whenever the tracking frame changes to the eyes/face of a different subject.

Manual Focus

Whenever it's difficult to properly focus on the autofocus mode, you could manually modify the focus.

1. MENU →Go to ^{AF}MF (Focus) → to [AF/MF] → [📷 Focus Mode] → [The Manual Focus].

2. Turn the focusing ring to get sharp focus.

- When still images are shot, the focus distance can be shown on the screen by turning the focusing ring. The focus distance isn't shown whenever the Mount Adaptor (not included) is connected.

Note

- When the viewfinder is used, modify the diopter level to get the appropriate focus on the viewfinder.
- The focus distance displayed is simply a reference.

Direct manual focus (DMF)

Fine adjustments can be manually made after carrying out auto focusing, allowing a subject to be focused on more quickly compared to when manual focus is used right from the start. This is ideal in situations like macro shooting.

1. Launch MENU→ Goto **AFMF** (Focus) →To [AF/MF] → [📷 Focus Mode] → [The DMF].

2. Focus automatically by pressing the shutter button partly down.

3. Leave the shutter button pushed partly down, and afterwards turn the focusing ring to get a sharper focus.

- When the focusing ring is rotated, the focus distance is shown on the screen. The focus distance isn't shown when the Mount Adaptor (not included) is connected.

4. Fully push the shutter button down to shoot the image.

SUBJECT RECOGNITION

The face/eye AF

Focus on human eyes

The product can automatically recognize eyes and faces as well as focus on the eyes (Eye AF). The explanation below is for instances where the target of detection is human. The faces of about 8 subjects can be recognized.

Item	[👤 Face/Eye Prior. in AF] function	[Eye AF] via a custom key
Characteristics	The camera will detect faces/eyes with greater priority.	The camera will detect faces/eyes exclusively.
Advance preparation	Select [👤 Face/Eye Prior. in AF] → [On]. Select [👤 Face/Eye Subject] → [Human].	Assign [Eye AF] to the desired key using [📷 Custom Key/Dial Set.] or [▶️ Custom Key/Dial Set.].

[Eye AF] can be performed using two methods with certain disparities between their specifications. Choose the suitable method in accordance with your purpose. How to perform [Eye AF]	Press the shutter button halfway down.*1	Press the key to which you have assigned the [Eye AF] function.*2

Function details	When the camera detects a face or eye inside or around the designated focus area, it focuses on the face or eye with greater priority. If the camera does not detect any faces or eyes inside or around the designated focus area, it will focus on another detectable subject.	The camera focuses exclusively on faces or eyes anywhere on the screen, regardless of the setting for [📷 Focus Area]. The camera will not automatically focus on another subject if no face or eye is detected anywhere on the screen.

Focus mode	Follows the setting designated with [📷 Focus Mode]	Follows the setting designated with [📷 Focus Mode]
Focus area	Follows the setting designated with [🎥 Focus Area]	The focus area temporarily becomes the entire screen, regardless of the setting for [🎥 Focus Area].

This operation is applicable for executing [Eye AF] when still images are shot. When shooting a movie, [Eye AF] is enabled without touching the shutter button inasmuch as eyes or faces are detected. Irrespective of whether [🎥 Face/Eye Prior. in AF] is put to [Off] or [On], [Eye AF] can be used through a custom key while you're touching the custom key that [Eye AF] has been assigned to.

[Eye AF] via custom key

This function can be used by designating [Eye AF] to a custom key. The product can focus on eyes inasmuch as the key is pressed.

This is relevant when the Eye AF function is to be temporarily applied to the whole screen irrespective of the setting for [🎥 Focus Area].

The product doesn't automatically focus if no eyes or faces are detected.

129

1. Launch MENU →Go to ⬛ (Setup) → [Operation Customise] → [▶⬛ Dial Set/Custom Key/] or [⬛ Custom Key/Dial Set.] → specific key, afterwards designate the [Eye AF] function to that key.

2. Launch MENU → **AF**_{MF} (Focus) → [Eye/Face AF] → [⬛ Face/Eye Subject] → [Human].

3. Direct the product at a human face, and touch the key that [Eye AF] function has been assigned to. To shoot still images, touch the shutter button while touching the key.

Focusing on the eyes of a bird or an animal

Configure [⬛ Eye Subject/Face] to [Bird] or [Animal] prior to shooting.

Hint

- Putting [⬛ Face/Eye Frame Disp.] to [On] makes checking the detection status of eyes or faces much easier.

Note

The [Eye AF] function might not properly function in the situations below:

- When the subject is putting on sunglasses.
- When the subject's eyes are covered by the front hair.
- In back-lit or low-light conditions.
- Whenever the eyes are shut.
- When the person is under the shade.

- When the person is out of focus.
- When the person moves too much

Other situations also exist where it might be impossible to focus on the eyes.

When the product can't focus on human eyes, it detects and focuses on the face instead. The camera can't focus on eyes whenever human faces aren't detected.

The camera might not detect faces in anyway or might mistakenly recognize other objects as faces under certain conditions.

Eye/Face Priority in AF (movie/still image)

Sets whether the product detects eyes or faces within the focus area while carrying out autofocus, and afterwards automatically focuses on the eyes (Eye AF).

1. MENU → ^{AF}MF (Focus) → [Face/Eye AF] → [🔲 Face/Eye Prior. in AF] → desired setting.

Menu options

- On: Prioritizes focus on the eyes or faces if there happen to be eyes or faces around or inside the specific focus area.
- Off: Doesn't prioritize eyes or faces when carrying out auto-focusing.

Hint

- Through the combination of the [📷 Focus Area] → [Tracking] with [📷 Face/Eye Prior. in AF] function, focus can be maintained on a moving face or eye.

- Whenever [Face/Eye Priority Select] is designated to the specific key via [▶ Custom Key/Dial Set.] or [📷 Custom Key/Dial Set.], the [📷 Face/Eye Prior. in AF] function can be switched off or on by touching the key.

- By designating [Face/Eye Prio. Off Tggle.] or [Face/Eye Prio. Off Hold] to the specific key using [📷 Custom Key/Dial Set.], [📷 Face/Eye Prior. in AF] can be temporarily switched to [Off] via the key.

Note

- If the product doesn't detect any eyes or faces around or inside the specific focus area, it focuses on a different detectable subject.
- Setting the shooting mode to [Intelligent Auto] locks [📷 Face/Eye Prior. in AF] to [On].

Eye/Face Subject (movie/still image)

Chooses the target to be identified with the Eye AF/Face function.

Launch MENU → **AF MF** (Focus) → [Face/Eye AF] → [📷 Face/Eye Subject] → desired setting.

Menu options

- **Human:** Recognizes human eyes/faces.
- **Animal:** Recognizes animal eyes.
- **Bird:** Recognizes the eyes of birds.

Hint

- To detect bird or animal eyes, the shot should be composed in such a way that the whole head is inside the viewing angle. Once the bird's or animal's head is focused on, detecting the eyes would be much easier.

Note

Whenever [📷 Face/Eye Subject] is put to [Bird] or [Animal], the below functions can't be used.

- Face Priority in Multi Metering
- Register Faces Priority

Even though [Face/Eye Subject] is put to [Animal], the eyes of certain kinds of animals can't be detected.

Even though [Face/Eye Subject] is put to [Bird], the eyes of certain kinds of birds can't be detected.

Subject Selection Setting (movie/still image)

Sets the kinds of detection targets available whenever the custom key assigned to [Swt Face/Eye Sbjc Dtc] is used.

1. MENU → **AF_{MF}** (Focus) → [Face/Eye AF] → [🔲 Subject Sel. Setting] → Checkmarks should be added to the desired detection targets, and afterwards choose [OK].

- The kinds of targets ticked with ✔ (check mark) would be available as settings.

Hint

- Designate [Swt Face/Eye Sbjc Dtc] to the specific key via [▶️ Custom Key/Dial Set.] or [📷 Custom Key/Dial Set.] or.
- You can choose the kinds of targets to which checkmarks are not added under [🔲 Subject Sel. Setting] by choosing MENU → **AF_{MF}** (Focus) → [Face/Eye AF] → [🔲 Face/Eye Subject].

Left/Right Eye Select (movie/still image)

Sets whether the right or left eye is to be focused on whenever [🐾 Face/Eye Subject] is put to [Animal] or [Human].

1. MENU → **AF**_{MF} (Focus) → [Face/Eye AF] → [🐾 Right/Left Eye Select] → desired setting.

Menu options

- Auto: The product automatically recognizes either the right eye or left eye.
- Right Eye: The subject's right eye (the eye at the left part from the viewpoint of the photographer) is detected.
- Left Eye: The subject's left eye (the eye at the right part from the viewpoint of the photographer) is detected.

[Switch Left/Right Eye] via custom key

The eye can also be switched to be detected by touching the custom key.

Whenever [🐾 Right/Left Eye Select] is put to [Left Eye] or [Right Eye], the eye can be switched to be recognized by touching the custom key that the [Switch Right/Left Eye] function has been assigned to.

Whenever [🐾 Right/Left Eye Select] is put to [Auto], the eye can be temporarily switched to be recognized by touching the custom key that the [Switch Right/Left Eye] function has been assigned to.

The temporary right/left selection is annulled whenever the below operations are performed, etc. The product goes back to automatic eye detection.

- Pressing the middle of the control wheel
- Pressing the middle of the multi-selector
- Stopping touching the shutter button partly down (only when shooting still images)
- Stopping touching the custom key to which [Eye AF] or [AF On] is designated (only when shooting still images)
- Touching the MENU button

Hint

- Whenever [🔳 Face/Eye Frame Disp.] is put to [On], the eye detection frame shows around the selected eye using [Switch Right/Left Eye] or [🔳 Right/Left Eye Select] with that custom key

Face/Eye Frame Display (movie/still image)

Sets whether the eye/face detection frame is to be displayed whenever eyes or faces are detected or not.

1. MENU → ^{AF}MF (Focus) → [Face/Eye AF] → [🔳 Face/Eye Frame Disp.] → desired setting.

Menu options

- **On**: Shows a detection frame whenever eyes or faces are detected.

136

- **Off**: Doesn't show a detection frame whenever eyes or faces are detected.

Face detecting frame

Whenever the product identifies a face, the gray face-detection frame shows. The color of the frame becomes reddish purple if the face detected was previously registered via the [Face Memory] function. The face detection frame becomes white whenever the face is identified around or inside the focus area, and the product ascertains that autofocus is activated.

Eye detecting frame

A white eye detection frame shows whenever an eye is identified and the product ascertains that it is possible to autofocus. The eye detection frame is shown as below whenever [📷 Face/Eye Subject] is put to [Bird] or [Animal].

Hint

If you want the face or eye detection frame to disappear within a certain period of time after the camera has focused on the face or eye, set [AF Area Auto Clear] to [On].

Note

If the subject happens to move around a lot, the detection frame might not be properly shown above their eyes. The eye detection frame isn't shown whenever the Eye AF function is not available.

Even though [🐾 Face/Eye Frame Disp.] is put to [Off], a green focusing frame appears over eyes or faces in focus whenever the shutter button is partly pressed down, etc.

Face Memory

This sets the individual's face data. If faces are registered beforehand, the camera prioritizes focus on the registered faces.

About 8 faces can be registered.

MENU → **AF**_{**MF**} (Focus) → [Face/Eye AF] → [Face Memory] → desired setting item.

Menu options

- New Registration. Shoots as well as register faces.
- Order Excng: Whenever several faces are registered, the order of priority for the data of registered faces can be altered.
- Delete: Registered faces are deleted one after the other.
- Delete All: All the registered faces are deleted at once.

Note

When carrying out [New Registration], the face should be shot from the front in a well-lit environment. The face might be incorrectly registered if it's blocked by sunglasses, a mask, a hat, etc.

Even if [Delete] is executed, the data for registered faces remains in the camera. To erase the registered face data from the camera, choose [Delete All].

Register Faces Priority (movie/still image)

Sets whether faces registered via [Face Memory] are to be focused on with higher priority.

1. MENU → ^{AF}MF (Focus) → [Face/Eye AF] → [🄰 Regist. Faces Priority] → desired setting.

Menu options

- On: Faces registered via [Face Memory] are focused on with higher priority.

- Off: Registered faces aren't given higher priority when focusing.

Hint

The [📷 Regist. Faces Priority] function can be used by setting as follows.

- [📷 Face/Eye Prior. in AF] below [Face/Eye AF]: [On]
- [📷 Face/Eye Subject] below [Face/Eye AF]: [Human]

USE FOCUSING FUNCTIONS

Focus Standard

If the button to which [Focus Standard] is designated is pressed, useful functions can be recalled like automatically focusing on subjects at the middle of the screen according to the settings for focus area.

1. MENU → 📷 (Setup) → [Operation Customize] → [▶️ Custom Key/Dial Set.] or [📷 Custom Key/Dial Set.] → desired key, afterwards designate the [Focus Standard] function to that key.

2. Touch the key [Focus Standard] is designated to.

- What can be done by touching the key differs contingent on the setting for [📷 Focus Area].

Instances of [Focus Standard] key functions

Whenever [📷 Focus Area] is put to any of the parameters below, touching the key returns the focusing frame to the middle of the monitor or to the subject being tracked:

- [Zone]
- [Spot: S]/[Spot: M]/[Spot: L]
- [Expand Spot]
- [Tracking: Zone]
- [Tracking: Spot L]/[Tracking: Spot M]/[Tracking: Spot S]
- [Tracking: Expand Spot]

Whenever [⚙ Focus Area] is put to [Tracking: Center Fix], [Tracking: Wide], [Center Fix], or [Wide], the product focuses on the middle of the screen when the key is pressed. If the key is pressed while recording movies using manual focus, you could temporarily change to autofocus and focus on the middle of the screen.

Note

The [Focus Standard] function cannot be set to [Down Button], [Right Button] or [Left Button] of the control wheel.

Adjust the settings for focus area in accordance with camera's orientation (vertical/horizontal) (Switch V/H AF Area)

You could set whether to change the [⚙ Focus Area] as well as the placement of the focusing frame in accordance with the camera's orientation (vertical/horizontal). This function comes in handy when scenes for which the position of the camera is to be frequently changed are shot, like sports scenes or portraits.

MENU → $^{AF}_{MF}$ (Focus) → [Focus Area] → [Switch V/H AF Area] → desired setting.

Menu options

- Off: Doesn't switch the placement of the focusing frame as well as the [📷 Focus Area] in accordance with the camera's orientation (vertical/horizontal).
- AF Point Only: Changes the placement of the focusing frame in accordance with the camera's orientation (vertical/horizontal). [📷 Focus Area] is fixed.
- AF Point + AF Area: Changes both the placement of the focusing frame as well as the [📷 Focus Area] in accordance with the camera's orientation (vertical/horizontal).

An instance of when [AF Point + AF Area] is chosen

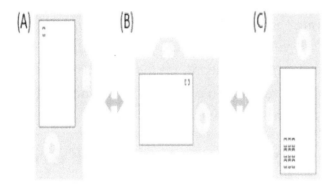

(A) Vertical: [Spot] (Top left corner)

(B) Horizontal: [Spot] (Top right corner)

(C) Vertical: [Zone] (Bottom left corner)

3. Camera orientations are identified: vertical with the shutter button's side facing upwards, vertical with shutter button's side facing downwards, and horizontal.

143

Note

Should the setting for [Switch V/H AF Area] be altered, the focus settings for all the camera orientation won't be retained.

The placement of the focusing frame as well as [📷 Focus Area] won't change even though [Switch V/H AF Area] is put to [AF Point Only] or [AF Point + AF Area] under the situations below:

- Whenever the shooting mode is put to [Intelligent Auto]
- While shooting a movie
- When the digital zoom function is being used
- When auto-focusing is enabled
- While shooting continuously
- When the self-timer is counting down
- Whenever [Focus Magnifier] is enabled
- When images are shot immediately after it's powered on and the product is vertical, the last focus setting or the horizontal focus setting is used in taking the first shot.
- The camera's orientation can't be identified whenever the lens is facing upwards or downwards

Register the present focus area (AF Area Registration)

The focusing frame can be temporarily moved to a pre-assigned position via a custom key. This function comes in handy when capturing scenes in which the movement of the subject is predictable; for instance, sports scenes. Using this function, the focus area can be quickly switched in accordance with the situation.

144

Registering focus area

1. MENU → **AF****MF** (Focus) → [Focus Area] → [AF Area Registration] → [On].

2. The focus area should be set to the specific position and afterwards the Fn (Function) button should be held down.

Calling up the focus area registered

1. MENU → 🧰 (Setup) → [Operation Customize] → [📷 Custom Key/Dial Set.] → specific key, afterwards choose [Regist. AF Area hold].

2. Set the product to the shooting mode, press down the button designated to [Regist. AF Area hold] and afterwards shoot images by pressing the shutter button.

Hint

Once a focusing frame is registered via [AF Area Registration], the registered frame blinks on the monitor.

If [Regist AF Area tggle] is assigned to a custom key, the registered focusing frame can be used without holding the key down.

If [Reg. AF Area+AF On] is designated to a custom key, auto focusing via that registered focusing frame is carried out whenever the key is pressed.

Note

A focus area can't be registered under the situations below:

- When [Touch Focus] is being carried out
- When the digital zoom function is being used

- When [Touch Tracking] is in progress
- During focusing
- When executing focus lock
- You can't designate [Regist. AF Area hold] to [Down Button], [Right Button], or [Left Button].

You can't call-up the registered focus area in the situations below:

- The Movie/S&Q/Still dial is put to either S&Q Motion (S&Q) or ▶■ (Movie)
- The mode dial is put to **AUTO** (Auto Mode)

Whenever [AF Area Registration] is put to [On], the settings for [Lock Operation Parts] is locked to [Off].

To delete a registered AF Area (Del. Register AF Area)

Erases the focusing frame position previously registered via [AF Area Registration].

MENU → ^{AF}**MF** (Focus) → [Focus Area] → [Del. Regist. AF Area].

Focus Area Limit (movie/still image)

Settings for [🐍 Focus Area] can be more quickly chosen when the kinds of focus area settings available are limited in advance.

MENU → ^{AF}**MF** (Focus) → [Focus Area] → [🐍 Focus Area Limit] → Checkmarks should be added to the desired focus areas, and afterwards choose [OK].

146

The kinds of focus areas ticked with ✔ (check mark) would be available as settings.

Hint

When [Switch Focus Area] is assigned to a particular key via [📷 Custom Key/Dial Set.] or [📷 Custom Key/Dial Set.], the focus area alters each time the designated key is pressed. By restricting the kinds of focus areas that can be selected with [📷 Focus Area Limit] beforehand, the desired focus area setting can be more quickly selected.

Note

Kinds of focus areas lacking checkmarks can't be selected via the function (Fn) menu or MENU. To choose one, add checkmark via [📷 Focus Area Limit].

If the checkmark is removed for the focus area registered via [AF Area Registration] or [Switch V/H AF Area], the settings registered would change.

Circ. of Focus Point (movie/still image)

Sets whether the focusing frame is to be allowed to move from one point to another when the focusing frame is moved. This function comes in handy when you'd like to quickly move the focusing frame from one point to another.

This function is applicable when the below settings are chosen for [![icon] Focus Area].

- [Zone]
- [Spot: L]/[Spot: S]/[Spot: M]
- [Expand Spot]
- [Tracking: Zone]
- [Tracking: Spot L]/[Tracking: Spot S]/[Tracking: Spot M]
- [Tracking: Expand Spot]

1. MENU →Go to **AF MF** (Focus) → [The Focus Area] → [![icon] Circ. Of The Focus Point] → needed setting.

When [Circulate] is chosen:

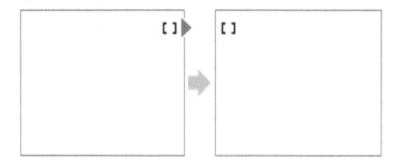

Menu options

- **Does Not Circulate**: The cursor doesn't move whenever you attempt to get the focusing frame beyond the end.

- **Circulate**: The cursor moves to the opposing end whenever you attempt to get the focusing frame beyond the end.

Note

Even if [⬛ Circ. of Focus Point] is set to [Circulate], the focusing frame won't circulate diagonally.

AF Frame Move Amount (movie/still image)

This determines the distance through which the focusing frame moves whenever [⬛ Focus Area] is put to [Spot], etc. The focusing frame can be quickly moved by increasing the distance, like in situations where subjects move a lot.

1. MENU → ^{AF}MF (Focus) → [Focus Area] → [⬛ AF Frame Move Amt] → desired setting.

Menu options

- Standard: The focusing frame is moved by the standard distance.
- Large: The focusing frame is moved over greater distances per time compared to [Standard].

Hint

Whenever [Swt. AF Frame Move hold] is designated to the specific key via [⬛ Custom Key/Dial Set.] or [⬛ Custom Key/Dial Set.], the setting for [📷 AF Frame Move Amt] temporarily changes while the button is pressed.

If any of the functions below is designated to the control wheel or dials via [▶📷 Custom Key/Dial Set.] or [📷 Custom Key/Dial Set.], the focusing frame can be moved through the distance set for each of the functions, irrespective of the setting for [📷 AF Frame Move Amt].

[Move AF Frame ←→ : L]

[Move AF Frame ↕ : L]

[Move AF Frame ←→ : Std]

[Move AF Frame ↕ : Std]

If any of the functions below is designated to the control wheel or dials via [My Dial Settings], the focusing frame can be moved through the distance set for each of the functions, irrespective of the setting for [📷 AF Frame Move Amt].

[Move AF Frame ←→ : L]

[Move AF Frame ↕ : L]

[Move AF Frame ←→ : Std]

[Move AF Frame ↕ : Std]

Focus Area Color (movie/still image)

The color of the frame outlining the focusing area can be specified. If it's difficult to see the frame as a result of the subject, change its color to increase its visibility.

1. MENU → **AF**MF (Focus) → [Focus Area] → [🔲 Focus Area Color] → specific color.

Menu options

- White: The frame outlining the focus area is displayed in white.

Red: The frame outlining the focus area is displayed in red.

AF Area Automatic Clear

Sets if the focus area is to be displayed every time or automatically disappear a little while after focus is attained whenever [🔲 Focus Mode] is put to [Single-shot AF].

1. MENU → **AF**MF (Focus) → [Focus Area] → [AF Area Auto Clear] → desired setting.

Menu options

On: The focus area automatically disappears briefly after focus is attained.

Off: The focus area is shown every time.

Area Displayed during Tracking

Sets if the frame for the focus area is to be displayed or not whenever [🔲 Focus Mode] is put to [Continuous AF] and [🔲 Focus Area] is put to [Tracking].

1. MENU →Go to **AF**MF (Focus) → [The Focus Area] → [Area Displayed. during Tracking] → specific setting.

Menu options

- On: The frame for the focusing area is displayed during tracking. Since the tracking start area is shown while the subject is being tracked, it's helpful when the next shooting session is about to begin.
- Off: Doesn't show the frame for the focusing area while tracking.

AF-C Area Display

You could set whether the area under focus is to be displayed or not whenever [📷 Focus Mode] is put to [Continuous AF] and [📷 Focus Area] is put to [Zone] or [Wide].

1. MENU → **AF**MF (Focus) → [Focus Area] → [AF-C Area Display] → needed setting.

Menu options

On: Shows the focus area under focus.

Off: Doesn't show the focus area under focus.

Note

Whenever [📷 Focus Area] is put to any of the options below, the focusing frames within the area under focus turns green:

- [Center Fix]
- [Spot]
- [Expand Spot]

Phase Detection Area

Sets whether the Phase Detection AF area is to be displayed or not.

1. MENU → **AF_{MF}** (Focus) → [Focus Area] → [Phase Detect. Area] → desired setting.

Menu options

- On: The Phase Detection AF area is displayed.
- Off: The Phase Detection AF area is not displayed.

Note

- Phase Detection AF is only available with supported lenses. If incompatible lens are attached, you'll not be able to make use of Phase Detection AF. Phase Detection AF might not function even with certain compatible lenses, like lenses previously bought and yet to be updated. For information on compatible lenses, check out Sony website in your area, or check a Sony dealer or a local authorized Sony service facility.
- When shooting pictures via the full-frame-size-compatible lens, the Phase Detection AF area won't be shown even though [Phase Detect. Area] is put to [On].
- When movies are being recorded, the Phase Detection AF area won't be displayed.

The AF Tracking Sensor

The AF track sensitivity can be selected whenever the subject goes out of focus under still image mode.

MENU → **AF**_{MF} (Focus) → [AF/MF] → [AF Tracking Sensitivity] → desired setting.

Menu options

- **5(Responsive)/4/3(Standard)/2/1(Locked on):** Choose [5(Responsive)] to responsively focus on subjects at varying distances.

Choose [1(Locked on)] to retain the focus on the particular subject whenever other objects are crossing the subject's front.

AF Transition Speed

This sets the focusing speed whenever the target of the auto focus is changed while shooting a movie.

MENU → **AF**_{MF} (Focus) → [AF/MF] → [AF Transition Speed] → desired setting.

Menu options

7 (Fast)/6/5/4/3/2/1 (Slow):

Choose a faster value in order to focus more quickly on the subject.

Choose a slower value in order to focus more smoothly on the subject.

Hint

- The touch focus function can be used to deliberately transition the AF.

AF Subject/object Shift Sensitivity

This sets the sensitivity with which the focus changes to a different subject whenever the initial subject goes out of the focus area or a previously unfocused subject in the foreground reaches the middle of the focus area while shooting a movie.

MENU → **AF MF** (Focus) → [AF/MF] → [AF Subj. Shift Sensitivity] → specific setting.

Menu options

5(Responsive)/4/3/2/1(Locked on):

Choose higher values whenever you need to shoot a fast-moving subject, or whenever you need to shoot several subjects while continually changing the focus.

Choose lower values whenever you need the focus to stay steady, or whenever the focus is to be kept on a certain subject without getting affected by the other subject.

AF Assist

When shooting movies using auto focus, the subject under focus can be quickly changed by using the lens' focus ring.

1. MENU → **AF MF** (Focus) → [AF/MF] → [AF Assist] → [On].

2. When shooting movies using auto focus, rotate the lens' focus ring to focus on the desired subject.

- Once the focus ring is no longer being operated, the subject under focus via the focus ring becomes the autofocus target.

Menu options

- On: The AF assist function is used.
- Off: The AF assist function is not used.

Hint

- Viewing the region under focus becomes easier when [Focus Map] function or [📷 Peaking Display] is used alongside [AF Assist]; this makes it easier to focus on the desired subject.

Note

- Only subjects inside the focus area are focused on by auto focus.
- The lenses below are incompatible with [AF Assist].

AF/MF Selector

The focusing mode can be easily switched from manual to auto and conversely when taking shots without changing the holding position.

MENU → 🧰 (Setup) → [Operation Customise] → [▶️📷 Custom Key/Dial Set.] or [📷 Dial Set./Custom Key] → needed button → [AF/MF Select Hold] or [AF/MF Select Toggle].

Menu options

- AF/MF Select Hold: The focusing mode is switched while the key is held down.
- AF/MF Select Toggle: The focusing mode is switched till the key is pressed a second time.

Note

- The [AF/MF Select Hold] function cannot be set to [Down Button], [Right Button], or [Left Button] of the control wheel.

AF w/ Shutter

Chooses whether to automatically focus whenever the shutter button is partly pressed down. Choose [Off] to separately change the exposure and the focus.

1. MENU →Go to **AF MF** (Focus) → [The AF/MF] → [AF w/ Shutter] → specific setting.

Menu options

- On: The auto focus functions whenever the shutter button is partly pressed down.
- Off: The auto focus doesn't function even if the shutter button is partly pressed down.

AF On

The focus can be changed without pushing the shutter button partly down. The settings for [Focus Mode] are applicable.

1. Touch the AF-ON button when shooting.

- When shooting movies, auto-focusing can be performed while the AF-ON button is held down even under the manual focusing mode.

Hint

- Put [AF w/ Shutter] to [Off] whenever you don't want to carry out auto focusing via the shutter button.
- Put [Pre-AF] and [AF w/ Shutter] to [Off] to focus at a particular shooting distance estimating the subject's position.

Focus Hold

The focus is locked while the button to which the Focus Hold function is designated is pressed.

1. MENU → (Setup) → [Operation Customize] → [Custom Key/Dial Set.] or [Custom Key/Dial Set.] → designate the [Focus Hold] function to the specific key.

2. Focus and touch the key assigned to the [Focus Hold] function.

Pre-AF

The camera automatically modifies focus prior to you pressing the shutter button partly down.

1. MENU → **AF**_{**MF**} (Focus) → [AF/MF] → [Pre-AF] → specific setting.

Menu options

- On: Focus is adjusted before the shutter button is pressed partly down.
- Off: Focus is not adjusted prior to the shutter button being pressed partly down.

Note

- [Pre-AF] is only available whenever an E-mount lens is mounted.
- In the course of focusing operations, the screen might shake.

The Priority Settings in AF-S

Sets whether the shutter is to be released even though the subject isn't in focus whenever [📷 Focus Mode] is put to [Automatic AF], [DMF], or [Single-shot AF] and the subject is standing still.

1. MENU → **AF**_{**MF**} (Focus) → [AF/MF] → [Priority Settings in AF-S] → specific setting.

Menu options

- **AF**: Focusing is prioritized. The shutter won't be released till the subject is being focused on.

159

- **Release**: The shutter's release is released. The shutter would be released even though the subject isn't in focus.
- **Balanced Emphasis:** Shots are taken with balanced emphasis on both shutter release and focusing.

Priority Settings in AF-C

Sets whether the shutter is to be released even though the subject isn't in focus whenever the continuous AF is enabled and the subject is moving.

1. MENU → **AF_{MF}** (Focus) → [AF/MF] → [Priority Set in AF-C] → specific setting.

Menu options

- AF: Focusing is prioritized.
- Release: The shutter's release is released. The shutter would be released even though the subject isn't in focus.
- Balanced Emphasis: Shots are taken with balanced emphasis on both shutter release and focusing.

AF Illuminator

This provides fill light to make focusing on subjects in dark areas much easier. Within the time it takes to partly press the shutter button down as well as lock focus, the AF illuminator comes on to let the product focus more easily. If the flash connected to the Multi Interface Shoe has the AF illuminator function, whenever the flash turns on, the flash's AF illuminator will also turn on.

1. MENU → **AF_{MF}** (Focus) → [AF/MF] → [The AF Illuminator] → specific setting.

Menu options

- Auto: The AF illuminator automatically lights up in dark places.
- Off: The AF illuminator is not used.

Note

The [AF Illuminator] cannot be used in the situations below:

- Whenever the shooting mode is [S&Q Motion] or [Movie].
- Whenever [🎦 Focus Mode] is put to [Automatic AF] or [Continuous AF] and the subject is in motion (whenever the focus indicator (⦿) / (( )) comes on).
- Whenever [Focus Magnifier] is enabled.
- Whenever a Mount Adaptor is connected.

The AF illuminator releases an extremely bright light. Though there isn't health hazard, don't look straight into the AF illuminator at close ranges.

Aperture Drive in AF

The aperture drive system is changed to give priority to silence or to the auto-focusing tracking performance.

1. MENU → $^{AF}_{MF}$ (Focus) → [AF/MF] → [Aperture Drive in AF] → specific setting.

Menu options

- Focus Priority: The aperture drive system is changed to give priority to auto-focusing performance.
- Standard: The standard aperture drive system is used.

161

- Silent Priority: The aperture drive system is changed to give priority to silence to make the sound of the aperture driver more quiet compared to [Standard].

Note

- Whenever [Focus Priority] is chosen, the aperture drive sound might be audible, or the aperture effect might be invisible on the monitor. To prevent these occurrences, alter the setting to [Standard].
- Whenever [Silent Priority] is chosen, the focusing speed might get slower, and focusing on subjects might be more difficult.
- The effect might vary contingent on the lens in use as well as the shooting conditions.

AF in Focus Magnification

The subject can be more precisely focused on via auto-focus by enlarging the region to be focused on. While the enlarged picture is shown, you could focus on smaller areas than [Spot] below [📷 Focus Area].

1. MENU → ^{AF}MF (Focus) → [The Focus Assistant] → [AF in Focus Mag.] → [On].

2. MENU → ^{AF}MF (Focus) → [Focus Assistant] → [Focus Magnifier].

3. Enlarge the picture by touching the middle of the multi-selector, and afterwards modify the position by touching the multi-selector right/left/down/up. The scale of magnification is changed every time the centre is pressed.

4. Partly push the shutter button downwards to focus. The focus is achieved at the point of plus mark (+) in the middle of the screen.

5. Shoot by fully pressing the shutter button down.

The product exits the enlarged display after the shoot.

Hint

- Use of tripods is advised to precisely identify the place to be magnified.
- The result of auto-focusing could be checked by enlarging the displayed picture. If you'd like to re-adjust the focus position, modify the focus area on the enlarged screen and afterwards partly push the shutter button down.

Note

- If a region at the screen's edge is enlarged, the camera might be unable to focus.
- The white balance and exposure can't be altered while the displayed picture is being enlarged.

[AF in Foc. Mag.] is not available in the situations below:

- While shooting a movie
- Whenever [📷 Foc. Mode] is put to [Continuous AF].
- Whenever [📷 Foc. Mode] is put to [Automatic AF] and shooting mode is put to apart from P/A/S/M.
- Whenever [📷 Foc. Mode] is put to [Automatic AF] and [Drive Mode] is put to [Cont. Shooting].
- When a Mount Adaptor is used (not included).

While the displayed picture is being enlarged, the functions below are not available:

- The Eye AF
- The Pre-AF
- The Face/Eye Prior. In AF

Automatic Magnification in Manual Focus

Automatically magnifies the picture on the screen to make manual focusing much easier. This is applicable in Direct Manual Focus or Manual Focus shooting.

1. MENU → **AF_{MF}** (Focus) → [Focus Assistant] → [Auto Magnifier in MF] → [On].

2. Rotate the focus by turning the focus ring.

The picture is magnified. Images can be further magnified by touching the middle of the control wheel.

Hint

- The duration for which the magnified picture is to be displayed can be set by choosing MENU → **AF_{MF}** (Focus) → [The Foc. Assistant] → [🎬 Foc. Magnify. Time].

Note

- [Auto Magnifier in MF] cannot be used when shooting a movie. The [Focus Magnifier] function should be used instead.

164

- [Auto Magnifier in MF] is unavailable whenever a Mount Adaptor is connected. The [Focus Magnifier] function should be used instead.

Focus Magnifier

The focus can be checked by magnifying the image prior to shooting. Compared with [Auto Magnifier in MF], the image can be magnified without using the focus ring.

1. MENU → **AF** **MF** (Focus) → [Focus Assistant] → [Focus Magnifier].

2. Press the middle of the multi-selector to magnify the picture and choose the area to be enlarged by pushing the multi-selector right/left/down/up.

Every time the center is pressed, the scale of magnification changes.

The initial magnification can be set by choosing MENU → **AF** **MF** (Focus) → [Focus Assistant] → [▶■ Initial Focus Mag.] or [🔲 Initial Foc. Mag.].

3. Affirm the focus.

Press the Delete (🗑) button to bring the enlarged position into the middle of a picture.

Whenever the focus mode is [Manual Focus], the focus can be adjusted while the image is enlarged. If [AF in Focus Mag.] is put to [Off], the [Focus Magnifier] function is annulled whenever the shutter button is halfway pressed down.

Whenever the shutter button is partly pressed down while a picture is enlarged during auto-focusing, various functions are executed contingent on the setting for [AF in Focus Mag.].

- Whenever [AF in Focus Mag.] is put to [On]: Auto-focusing is executed again.
- Whenever [AF in Focus Mag.] is put to [Off]: The [Focus Magnifier] function is annulled.

The duration for which a picture is to be displayed magnified can be set by choosing MENU → $^{AF}_{MF}$ (Focus) → [Focus Assistant] → [📷 Focus Magnif. Time].

Using the focus magnifier function via touch operation

The image can be magnified and the focus adjusted by tapping the monitor. Put [Touch Operation] to [On] in advance. Afterwards, choose the suitable settings below [Touch Panel/Pad]. Whenever the focus mode is [Manual Focus], [Focus Magnifier] can be performed by double-clicking the area to be focused on while taking shot via the monitor.

When shooting via the viewfinder, a frame is shown in the middle of the monitor by double-clicking and the frame can be moved by pulling it. The picture is enlarged by touching the middle of the multi-selector.

Hint

- When the focus magnifier function is in use, the enlarged area can be moved by pulling it via the touch pad.

- To quit the focus magnifier function, double-click the monitor a second time. Whenever [AF in Focus Mag.] is put to [Off], the focus magnifier function gets ended when the shutter button is partly pressed down.

Focus Magnification Time

The duration for which images are to be magnified can be set via the [Focus Magnifier] or [Auto Magnifier in MF] function.

1. MENU → **AF**MF (Focus) → [The Focus Assistant] → [📷 Focus Magnify. Time] → specific setting.

Menu options

- 2 Sec: Images are magnified for two seconds.
- 5 Sec: Images are magnified for five seconds.
- No Limit: Images are magnified till the shutter button is pressed.

Initial Focus Magnification (movie)

This sets the initial magnification scale for [Focus Magnifier] under movie shooting mode.

1. MENU → **AF**MF (Focus) → [Focus Assistant] →[Initial Focus Mag.] → specific setting.

Menu options

- x1.0: The image is displayed with magnification similar to that of the shooting screen.
- x4.0: A 4.0-times magnified image is displayed.

Focus Map

When shooting movies, areas under focus as well as areas out of focus are shown so that they can be visually distinguished. Areas at the back of the areas in focus area are outlined by dots in cool colors (A) and those at the front of the areas in focus are outlined by dots in warm colors (B). Dots aren't shown in the in-focus range. Dots aren't recorded in the real movie.

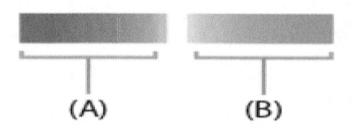

(A)   (B)

1. MENU → **AF** **MF** (Focus) → [Focus Assistant] → [Focus Map] → specific setting.

Menu options

- On: The focus map is displayed.
- Off: The focus map is not displayed.

Hint

- The focus map could also be output to external monitors. The focus map can be output to external monitors by setting [HDMI Info. Display] to [On].

Note

[Focus Map] isn't available in the situations below:

- Whenever [Focus Magnifier] is enabled

168

- When the digital zoom function is in use
- When performing [USB Streaming]
- When a lens that is incompatible with phase detection AF is used
- Whenever Mount Adaptors are attached
- Whenever the lens isn't connected to the product

Peaking Display

When shooting with Direct Manual Focus or Manual Focus, this sets the peaking function, which improves the outline of areas in focus. When shooting movies, the peaking function can also be used alongside auto focus.

1. MENU → **AF MF** (Focus) → [Peaking Display] → Choose a menu item and put the needed parameter.

Menu options

🔛 Peaking Display: Sets if peaking is to be displayed or not. ([On] / [Off])

🔛 Peaking Level: Sets the degree of enhancement of the areas in focus. ([High] / [Mid] / [Low])

🔛 Peaking Color: Chooses the color used in enhancing in-focus regions. ([White] / [Blue] / [Yellow] / [Red])

Note

Since the camera recognizes sharp regions as under focus, the impact of peaking varies, contingent on the lens and subject.

The outline of ranges in focus isn't improved on gadgets connected through HDMI.

Adjust the metering mode/ exposure

Exposure Comp. (movie/still image)

Ordinarily, exposure is determined automatically (auto-exposure). Depending on the exposure value determined by auto-exposure, the entire picture can be made darker or brighter if [📷 Exposure Comp.] is adjusted to the minus side or plus side, respectively (exposure compensation).

1. MENU → 🔲 (Exposure/Color) → [Exposure Comp.] → [📷 Exposure Comp.] → specific setting.

- + (over) side: Pictures become brighter.
- - (under) side: Pictures become darker.

[📷 Exposure Comp.] is designated to the rear dial R under default settings. Exposure compensation can also be set by unlocking and rotating the rear dial R. Touching the lock button at the middle changes the rear dial R between the unlocked and locked status. Whenever the lock button pops up and the white line is obvious, the dial is unlocked.

The exposure compensation value can be adjusted in the ranges of +5.0 EV to -5.0 EV.

The exposure compensation value so set can be confirmed on the screen for shooting.

The Monitor

The Viewfinder

Hint

Only values in the range of +3.0 EV and -3.0 EV alongside the corresponding picture brightness shows on the screen during shoots. If exposure compensation values are set beyond this range, the brightness of the image on the screen won't be influenced, but that value would be reflected on the recorded picture.

The exposure compensation value can be adjusted in the ranges of +2.0 EV to -2.0 EV for movies.

Note

Exposure compensation cannot be performed in the shooting modes below:

- [Intelligent Auto]
- Whenever [Manual Exposure] is in use, exposure compensation can only be performed when [ISO] is put to [ISO AUTO].
- If subjects are shot in extremely dark or bright conditions, or when the flash is used, you might be unable to get satisfactory effects.

HISTOGRAM DISPLAY

This depicts the luminance distribution, showing the number of pixels present by luminance.

To show the histogram on the playback or shooting screen, repeatedly touch the Display Setting (DISP) button.

Reading the histogram

On the histogram, darker values are indicated leftwards and brighter values rightwards.

The histogram modifies based on the exposure compensation.

A peak towards the left or right part of the histogram denotes that the picture has an underexposed or overexposed area, respectively. Such defects can't be corrected via a computer after the shot has been taken. Exposure compensation should be performed prior to shooting as required.

(A): Pixel count

(B): Brightness

Note

- The info on the histogram display in no way indicates the final picture. It is info about picture shown on the screen. The end result is contingent on the aperture value, etc.

The histogram display is very different between playback and shooting in the cases below:

- Whenever the flash is used
- When low luminance subjects are shot like night scenes

Metering Mode

The standard value set would be applied whenever the corresponding metering mode is selected in MENU →  (Exposure/Color) → [Metering] → [📷 Metering Mode].

📷⁺ Highlight / ▣ Entire Screen Average/ ▣ Spot/ ◉ Center/ ▣ Multi

Note

- The exposure compensation won't be affected whenever [📷 Exposure Std. Adjust] is altered.
- The exposure value would be locked in accordance with the set value for [▣ Spot] when making use of spot AEL.
- The standard value for Metered Manual (M.M) would be changed in accordance with the set value in [📷 Exposure Std. Adjust].

- The set value in [📷 Exposure Std. Adjust] is separately recorded in Exif data from the exposure compensation value. The degree of exposure standard value won't be added to the value of exposure compensation.
- If [📷 Exposure Std. Adjust] is set in the course of bracketing shooting, the amount of shots for the bracketing would be reset.

D-Range Optimizer (movie/still image)

By splitting the picture into small bits, the camera analyses the contrast of shadow and light between the background and the subject, and creates images using the optimal gradation and brightness.

1. MENU → 🔲 (Exposure/Color) → [Color/Tone] → [📷 D-Range Optimizer] → specific setting.

Menu options

- Off: Doesn't adjust gradation and brightness.
- D-Range Optimizer: If [D-Range Optimizer: Auto] is selected, the product will automatically alter the gradation and brightness. For the gradation of recorded images to be optimized by individual regions, choose a level of optimization within the ranges of [D-Range Optimizer: Lv5] (strong) and [D-Range Optimizer: Lv1] (weak).

Note

In the situations below, [📷 D-Range Optimizer] is set to [Off]:

- Whenever [📷 Picture Profile] is fixed to apart from [Off]
- When shooting via [D-Range Optimizer], the picture might be noisy. Choose the appropriate level by going through the recorded images, particularly when the effect is enhanced.

Metering Mode (movie/still image)

Chooses the metering mode which determines the part of the screen to be measured for ascertaining the exposure.

1. MENU → 🔲 (Exposure/Color) → [Metering] → [📷 Metering Mode] → specific setting.

Menu options

- 🔲 Multi: Light on every area is measured after the total area has been divided into several areas and the appropriate exposure of the whole screen is determined (Multi-pattern metering).
- 🔲 Center: The average brightness of the whole screen is measured, while the central part of the screen is emphasized (Center-weighted metering).
- 🔲 Spot: Only measures within the metering circle. This mode is appropriate for measuring light on particular parts of the whole screen. The dimension of the metering circle could be chosen from [Spot: Large] and [Spot: Standard]. The placement of the metering circle is dependent on the setting for [📷 Spot Metering Point].
- 🔲 Entire Screen Avg.: The average brightness of the whole screen is measured. The exposure would be stable even though the subject's position or composition changes.

176

- ⊡ Highlight: The brightness is measured while the highlighted part of the screen is emphasized. This mode is appropriate for shooting subjects while preventing overexposure.

Hint

- The spot metering point could be coordinated alongside the focus area through the use of [Focus Point Link].

- Whenever [Multi] is chosen and [📷 Face Priority in Multi Metering] is fixed to [On], the product measures brightness on the basis of detected faces.

- Whenever [📷 Metering Mode] is fixed to [Highlight] and the [D-Range Optimizer] function is enabled, the contrast and the brightness would be automatically corrected by splitting the picture into small regions as well as analysing the contrast of shadow and light. Settings can be made on the basis of shooting circumstances.

Note

[📷 Metering Mode] is locked at [Multi] in the shooting situations below:

- [Intelligent Auto]
- When zoom functions apart from optical zoom is used.
- Under [Highlight] mode, the subject might be dark if there happens to be a brighter part on the screen.

Spot Metering Point (movie/still image)

Sets whether the spot metering position is to be coordinated with the focus area whenever [📷 Focus Area] is put to the parameters below:

- [Spot: L]/[Spot: S]/[Spot: M]
- [Expand Spot]
- [Tracking: Spot L]/[Tracking: Spot S] /[Tracking: Spot M]
- [Tracking: Expand Spot]

1. MENU → ➕➖ (Exposure/Color) → [Metering] → [📷 Spot Metering Point] → specific setting.

Menu options

- **Center**: The spot metering position doesn't coordinate with focus area, but always meters brightness at the middle.
- **Focus Point Link:** The spot metering position synchronizes with the focus area.

Note

- Even though the spot metering position is synchronized with the [Tracking] start position, it won't be synchronized with the subject's tracking.
- Whenever [📷 Focus Area] is put to the parameters below, the spot metering position is locked at the middle.

> [Wide]
> [Zone]
> [Center Fix]
> [Tracking: Center Fix]/[Tracking: Wide]/[Tracking: Zone]

Face Priority in Multi Metering (movie/still image)

Sets whether brightness is to be measured by the camera on the basis of the faces detected whenever [Metering Mode] is fixed to [Multi].

MENU → ![Exposure/Color icon] (Exposure/Color) → [Metering] → [![icon] Face Priority in Multi Metering] → specific setting.

Menu options

- On: The product measures brightness on the basis of detected faces.
- Off: The product measures brightness via the [Multi] setting, without recognizing faces.

Note

- Whenever the shooting mode is put to [Intelligent Auto], [![icon] Face Priority in Multi Metering] is locked at [On].
- Whenever [![icon] Face/Eye Prior. in AF] is put to [On] and [![icon] Face/Eye Subject] is put to [Bird] or [Animal] below [Face/Eye AF], [![icon] Face Priority in Multi Metering] doesn't work.

AEL w/ Shutter

Sets whether the exposure is to be fixed whenever the shutter button is partly pressed down. Choose [Off] to separately adjust the exposure and the focus.

1. MENU → ![icon] (Exposure/Color) → [Metering] → [AEL w/ Shutter] → specific setting.

Menu options

- Auto: Sets the exposure after the focus is automatically adjusted whenever the shutter button is partly pressed down when [![icon] Focus Mode] is fixed to [Single-shot AF]. Whenever [![icon] Focus Mode] is fixed to [Automatic AF], and the camera ascertains that the subject is in motion, or burst images are shot, the fixed exposure is annulled.
- On: Sets the exposure whenever the shutter button is partly pressed down.
- Off: Doesn't set the exposure whenever the shutter button is partly pressed down. This mode should be used whenever you'd like to separately alter exposure and focus. The camera keeps altering the exposure when shooting via [Cont. Shooting] mode.

Note

- Operation via the AEL button is given priority over the settings for [AEL w/ Shutter] settings.

AE lock

Whenever the contrast between the background and the subject is high, like when shooting backlit subjects or subjects near windows, the light should be metered at the spot where the subject seems to have the suitable brightness and the exposure locked prior to shooting.

To lower the subject's brightness, the light should be metered at a spot brighter than the subject and the exposure of the whole screen locked. For the subject to be made brighter the light should be metered at a spot darker than the subject and the exposure of the whole screen locked.

1. Regulate the focus at the spot where the exposure is altered.

2. Touch the AEL button.

The exposure is locked, and ✳ (AE lock) is shown.

3. Keep touching the AEL button then focus on the subject a second time, afterwards shoot the image.

Continue holding the AEL button down while taking shots if you'd like to keep shooting using the fixed exposure. Reset the exposure by releasing the button.

Hint

If the [AEL toggle] function is assigned to the AEL button via [▶️■ Custom Key/Dial Set.] or [📷 Custom Key/Dial Set.], the exposure can be locked without having to hold the button down.

ADD EFFECTS TO IMAGES

Adjusting in greater detail

On the basis of each "Look," items like contrast can be altered to your preference. Both the pre-set "Looks" and each [Custom Look] can be adjusted; this function lets you register your preferred settings. Choose the item to be set by touching the left/right parts of the control wheel; afterwards fix the values using the bottom/top parts of the control wheel.

Whenever setting values are altered from the default value, asterisk (✱) is added beside the "Look" symbol shown on the shooting screen.

- **Contrast:** The greater the value chosen, the greater the difference of shadow and light is emphasized, and the greater the effect on the picture. (-9 to +9).

- **Highlights:** Alters the brightness of the bright places. Whenever higher values are selected, the picture gets brighter. (-9 to +9).

- **Shadows:** Alters the darkness of the dark places. When higher values are selected, the picture gets brighter. (-9 to +9).

- **Fade:** Alters the extent of fade. Larger values increase the effect. (0 to 9).

- **Saturation:** The vividness of the color is proportional to the value selected. Whenever lower values are chosen, the color of the picture is subdued and restrained. (-9 to +9).

- **⊞ Sharpness:** Alters the sharpness. The higher the value chosen, the more accentuated the contours are, and the lower the value chosen, the more softened the contours are. (0 to 9).

- **⬌ Sharpness Range:** Alters the range where the sharpness effect is added. Larger values make the sharpness effect add to finer outlines. (1 to 5).

- **▲ Clarity:** Alters the extent of clarity. Larger values increase the effect. (0 to 9)

Resetting adjusted values for every "Look"

Adjusted values like contrast that have been altered as preferred can be reset as a whole for every "Look." Touch the delete (🗑) button on the adjustment screen for the "Look" to be reset. All altered values that have been modified will go back to their default values.

Hint

- For [Clarity], [Sharpness Range], and [Sharpness], take test shots and either magnify and play it using the camera monitor, or output it to playback devices to see the effect. Afterwards, re-adjust the setting where needed.

Note

[Creative Look] is set to [ST] in the situations below:

- [Intelligent Auto]

- [Picture Profile] is fixed to apart from [Off].
- Whenever this function is fixed to [SE] or [BW], [Saturation] can't be adjusted.

Under movie mode, [Sharpness Range] can't be adjusted.

Creative Look (movie/still image)

"Looks" are pre-sets for image creation preloaded on the product.

Using this function, the finish of a picture can be selected by choosing a "Look". Additionally, you could fine-tune the clarity, sharpness range, sharpness, saturation, fade, shadows, highlights, and contrast for every "Look".

1. MENU → ![icon] (Exposure/Color) → [Color/Tone] → [![icon] Creative Look].

2. Choose the desired [Custom Look] or "Look" via the bottom/top of the control wheel.

3. To alter ▲ (Clarity), ![icon] (Sharpness Range), ![icon] (Sharpness), ![icon] (Saturation), ![icon] (Fade), ![icon] (Shadows), ![icon] (Highlights), and ![icon] (Contrast), move rightwards via the right part of the control wheel. Choose the needed item via the left/right sides, and afterwards choose the value via the bottom/top sides.

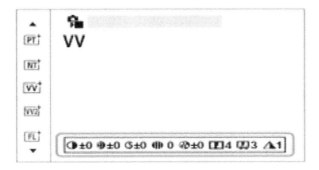

4. When choosing [Custom Look], move rightwards via the right part of the control wheel, and afterwards choose the needed "Look."

- Via [Custom Look], similar "Look" pre-sets can be recalled with a little different settings.

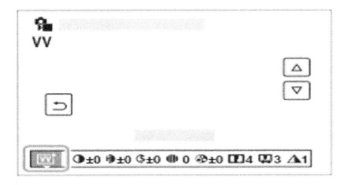

Menu options

- [ST] ST: Standard finish for a large range of scenes and subjects.
- [PT] PT: To capture skin in soft tones, best suited for taking portraits.
- [NT] NT: The sharpness and saturation are reduced for shooting pictures in subdued tones. This is also ideal for capturing image materials to be altered with computers.

- **VV⁺** VV: The contrast and saturation are increased for shooting impressive pictures of colorful subjects and scenes like ocean views, blue sky, spring greenery, or flowers.

- **VV2⁺** VV2: Creates images with vivid and bright colors with rich clarity.

- **FL⁺** FL: Creates images with moody finish by adding sharp contrasts to calm colorings in addition to the color of the greens and the impressive sky.

- **IN⁺** IN: Creates images with matte textures by subduing the saturation and contrast.

- **SH⁺** SH: Creates images with transparent, vivid, bright, and soft mood.

- **BW⁺** BW: For shooting pictures in black-and-white monotone.

- **SE⁺** SE: For shooting pictures in sepia monotone.

- **1SH⁺** Registering preferred settings (Custom Look): Choose the 6 custom look (the boxes with numbers at the left part) to register the particular settings. Afterwards choose the preferred settings via the right button.

- You could recall similar "Look" pre-sets with a little different setting.

Picture Profile (movie/still image)

Let's you alter the settings for the gradation, color etc.

Though [📷 Picture Profile] could be used for both movies and still images, the function was created for movies.

Customize the picture profile

The picture quality can be customized by altering picture profile items like [Detail] and [Gamma]. When fixing these parameters, attach the product to a monitor or TV, and alter them while looking at the image on the screen.

1. MENU → ⊞ (Exposure/Color) → [Color/Tone] → [📷 Picture Profile] → the profile to be changed.

2. Go to the item index screen by touching the right part of the control wheel.

3. Choose the item to be changed using the bottom/top parts of the control wheel.

4. Choose the preferred value using the bottom/top parts of the control wheel and push in the middle.

Use the pre-set picture profile

The default settings - [PP1] through [PP11] - for movies were set beforehand in the product based on different shooting conditions.

1. MENU → ⊞ (Exposure/Color) → [Color/Tone] → [📷 Picture Profile] → specific setting.

187

PP1: Example setting with [Movie] gamma.

PP2: Example setting with [Still] gamma.

PP3: Example setting of natural color tones with the [ITU709] gamma.

PP4: Example setting of color tones loyal to the ITU709 standard.

PP5: Example setting with [Cine1] gamma.

PP6: Example setting with [Cine2] gamma.

PP7: Example setting with [S-Log2] gamma.

PP8: Example setting with the [S-Gamut3.Cine] and the [S-Log3] gamma below [Color Mode].

PP9: Example setting with the [S-Gamut3] and the [S-Log3] gamma below [Color Mode].

PP10: Example settings to record HDR movies with [HLG2] gamma.

PP11: Example setting with [S-Cinetone] gamma.

SET THE RECORDING FORMAT AND IMAGE QUALITY

JPEG/HEIF Switch

Changes the file format (JPEG / HEIF) of the still image being recorded.

The JPEG format is generally compatible. JPEG files can be viewed and edited in different environments. The HEIF format has high compression efficiency. The product could record with small file sizes and high image quality under the HEIF format.

Contingent on the software or computer, you might be unable to edit or view HEIF files. Additionally, a HEIF-compatible environment is needed to playback still images under the HEIF format. High-quality still images can be enjoyed by attaching the product and the TV using HDMI.

1. MENU → 📷 (Shooting) → [Image Quality] → [JPEG/HEIF Switch] → specific setting.

Menu options

- JPEG: Carries out digital processing on the RAW file and records it via the JPEG format. This setting prioritizes compatibility.
- HEIF(4:2:0): Carries out digital processing on the RAW file and records it under the HEIF (4:2:0) format. This setting prioritizes compression efficiency and image quality.

- HEIF(4:2:2): Carries out digital processing on the RAW file and records it under the HEIF (4:2:2) format. This setting prioritizes image quality.

Hint

- Contingent on the settings for [JPEG/HEIF Switch], items connected to the file format ([File Format], etc.) would switch to HEIF or JPEG.

Note

- HEIF image files recorded using this product can't be shown on different cameras that are incompatible with the HEIF file format. Apply caution so as not to mistakenly delete HEIF image files by erasing the files or formatting the memory card.
- When recording via the HEIF format with [HLG Still Image] fixed to [Off], the color space is recorded in sRGB. Whenever [HLG Still Image] is fixed to [On], it's recorded under the BT.2100 color space (BT.2020 color gamut).

Image Quality Settings: File Format (still image)

Fixes the file format for still images.

1. MENU → (Shooting) → [Image Quality] → [Image Quality Settings] → [File Format] → specific setting.

Menu options

- RAW: The Digital processing isn't carried out on this file format. Choose this format to process pictures on computers for professional uses.
- RAW & HEIF/RAW & JPEG/: A RAW image as well as HEIF or JPEG image is created simultaneously. This is ideal when two image files are needed, a HEIF or JPEG for viewing, and a RAW for editing.
- JPEG/HEIF: Images are recorded using the HEIF or JPEG format.

Whenever [Recording Media] is fixed to [Sort Recording], the file format for both slots can be selected from amongst RAW and HEIF, or RAW and JPEG.

RAW images

To open RAW image files recorded using this product, the software Imaging Edge Desktop is required. Via Imaging Edge Desktop, RAW image files can be opened, afterwards converted into popular image formats like TIFF or JPEG, or the white balance readjusted, contrast or saturation of the picture.

RAW images recorded using this product have a res of 14 bits per pixel. Nevertheless, resolution is restricted to 12 bits in the shooting modes below:

[Cont. Shooting] whenever [RAW File Type] is fixed to [Compressed]

The method of compression for RAW images can be set via [RAW File Type].

Note

- If you don't plan on editing the pictures on a computer, we advise that recording be done in HEIF or JPEG format.
- An environment compatible with HEIF format is needed to playback HEIF images.

Image Quality Settings: RAW File Type

Chooses the file type for RAW images.

1. MENU → 📷 (Shooting) → [Image Quality] → [Image Quality Settings] → [RAW File Type] → specific setting.

Menu options

- Uncompressed: Images are recorded in uncompressed RAW format. Whenever [Uncompressed] is chosen for [RAW File Type], the image's file size would be larger compared to if recording was done via compressed RAW format.
- Lossless Comp: Records Images are recorded via the lossless compression method, which has a high compression rate and causes zero loss in image quality.
- Compressed: Images are recorded via the compressed RAW format. The image's file size would be about half of that with [Uncompressed].

Hint

The [RAW File Type] symbols are displayed as seen below.

- Uncompressed: **RAW**
- Lossless compression: **RAW**
- Compressed: **RAW**

192

RAW images have an aspect ratio of 3:2. JPEG/HEIF pictures are recorded with the aspect ratio fixed in [Aspect Ratio] whenever RAW images as well as JPEG/HEIF images are recorded simultaneously.

The image size for RAW pictures correlates to the "L" size for JPEG pictures.

Note

RAW images cannot be recorded with varying formats to Slot 1 and 2. Even though [📷 Recording Media] is fixed to [Sort Recording], both slots have similar settings for [RAW File Type].

Image Quality Set: HEIF Quality/ JPEG Quality

Chooses the image quality when recording HEIF or JPEG images.

1. MENU → 📷 (Shooting) → [Image Quality] → [Image Quality Settings] → [JPEG Quality]/[HEIF Quality] → specific setting.

Menu options

- Fine/ Extra fine/Light/ Standard: Seeing that the rate of compression increases from [Extra fine] to [Fine] to [Standard] to [Light], file size reduces following that order. This permits the recording of more files on a memory card, but with a lower image quality.

- Whenever [📷 Recording Media] is fixed to [Sort Recording], the image quality can be selected for each of the slots.

Aspect Ratio

1. MENU → [📷] (Shooting) → [Image Quality] → [Aspect Ratio] → specific setting.

Menu options

3:2: Similar aspect ratio to 35 mm film

4:3: The aspect ratio is 4:3.

16:9: The aspect ratio is 16:9.

1:1: The aspect ratio is 1:1.

Image Quality Set: HEIF Image Size/ JPEG Image Size

The bigger the image size, the more details reproduced whenever the picture is printed using large-format paper. The smaller the image size, the more pictures recordable.

1. MENU → [📷] (Shooting) → [Image Quality] → [Image Quality Settings] → [JPEG Image Size]/[HEIF Image Size] → specific setting.

Menu options

- Whenever [Aspect Ratio] is fixed to 3:2

Setting values	Pixel number (horizontal×vertical)
L: 33M	7008×4672 pixels
M: 14M	4608×3072 pixels
S: 8.2M	3504×2336 pixels

- Whenever [Aspect Ratio] is fixed to 4:3

Setting values	Pixel number (horizontal×vertical)
L: 29M	6224×4672 pixels
M: 13M	4096×3072 pixels
S: 7.3M	3120×2336 pixels

- Whenever [Aspect Ratio] is fixed to 16:9

Setting values	Pixel number (horizontal×vertical)
L: 28M	7008×3944 pixels
M: 12M	4608×2592 pixels
S: 6.9M	3504×1968 pixels

- Whenever [Aspect Ratio] is fixed to 1:1

Setting values	Pixel number (horizontal×vertical)
L: 22M	4672×4672 pixels
M: 9.4M	3072×3072 pixels
S: 5.5M	2336×2336 pixels

Hint

- Whenever recording is done via the M or S size, the pixel number won't change even though the viewing angle is switched between the APS-C and full-frame size.

Note

- The L size can't be chosen whenever APS-C size is used in shooting. If shots are taken using the APS-C size while L size is chosen, the image size would temporarily change to the M size.

HLG Still Image

Through the use of gamma characteristics corresponding to HLG (Hybrid Log-Gamma: standard for HDR images), still images can be shot using a wide color gamut as well as a wide dynamic range that supports BT.2020.

[HLG Still Image] can only be fixed whenever shooting is done using the HEIF format. Fix [JPEG/HEIF Switch] to [HEIF(4:2:2)] or

[HEIF(4:2:0)], and [File Format] below [Image Quality Settings] to [HEIF] in advance.

MENU → (Shooting) → [Image Quality] → [HLG Still Image] → specific setting.

Menu options

- On: The HLG still image is shot
- Off: Normal still image is shot

Hint

- A wider brightness range can be reproduced through the playback of HLG still images on an HLG-compatible monitor or TV.
- You can show HLG still images on the product's monitor in a quality almost the same as when they are shown on an HLG- (BT.2020-) compatible monitor by fixing as follows.

- [Gamma Display Assist]: [On]
- [Gamma Disp. Assist Typ.]: [HLG(BT.2020)] or [Auto]

Note

In the situations below, [HLG Still Image] is set to [Off]:

[JPEG/HEIF Switch] is fixed to [JPEG]

[File Format] below [Image Quality Settings] is fixed to [RAW & HEIF] or [RAW]

Whenever shooting mode apart from P / A / S / M is fixed in the course of still image shooting

Whenever ISO sensitivity is temporarily enabled by the [Reg. Custom Shoot Set] function

Whenever the [DRO Bracket] function below [Drive Mode] is temporarily enabled by the [Reg. Custom Shoot Set] function

Whenever [HLG Still Image] is fixed to [On], the functions below are unavailable.

- [D-Range Optimizer]
- [📷 Creative Look]
- [DRO Bracket] under [Drive Mode]
- [📷 Picture Profile]

Whenever [HLG Still Image] is fixed to [On], available ISO range alters.